The Rabbit

Howell Book House

Wiley Publishing, Inc.

Howell Book House
Published by Wiley Publishing, Inc., Hoboken, NJ
Published simultaneously in Canada

For general information about our other products and services, please contact our Customer Care Department within the United States at (800) 762-2974, outside the United States at (317) 572-3993 or fax (317) 572-4002.

Wiley also publishes its books in a variety of electronic formats. Some content that appears in print may not be available in electronic books. For more information about Wiley products, visit our web site at www.wiley.com.

Library of Congress Cataloging-in-Publication data
Pavia, Audrey
The rabbit: an owner's guide to a happy healthy pet/by Audrey Pavia.
p. cm.
Includes bibliographical references.
ISBN 0-87605-489-0
1. Rabbits as pets. I. Title.
SF453.P38 1996, 2001 96-21903
636.9322—dc20 CIP

Manufactured in the United States of America

18 17 16 15 14

Second Edition

Series Director: Kira Sexton
Book Design: Michele Laseau
Cover Design: Michael Freeland
Photography Editor: Richard Fox
Illustration: Ryan Oldfather
Photography:
Front and back cover photos by © Ron Kimball Studios
ARBA: 24, 26, 30, 36
Joan Balzarini: 31, 66, 74, 87, 94, 113
Paulette Braun/Pets by Paulette: 7, 15, 19, 25, 72, 73, 107
Adam Gaus: 22, 27, 28, 33
Audrey Pavia: 117
Cheryl Primeau: 49
Renée Stockdale: 5, 11, 12, 18, 20, 21, 32, 38, 42, 44, 45, 46, 51, 52, 54, 56, 57, 59, 60, 61, 63, 64, 65, 67, 68, 71, 75, 77, 78, 80, 81, 82, 83, 86, 88, 89, 92, 93, 95, 98, 99, 102, 103, 104, 106, 108, 109, 110, 111
Faith Uridel: 14, 23, 29, 35, 84, 114, 115
Jean Wentworth: 6, 9
WB/Phototest: 9
Production Team: Kathleen Caulfield, Michelle Croninger, and Chris Van Camp

Contents

part one

Welcome to the World of the Rabbit

1 History of the Rabbit 5

2 Rabbits as Pets 11

3 Rabbit Breeds 21

part two

Living with a Rabbit

4 Bringing Bunny Home 42

5 Indoor Rabbits 57

6 Outdoor Rabbits 66

7 Nutrition and Grooming 75

8 Your Rabbit's Health 86

part three

Enjoying Your Rabbit

9 Understanding Your Rabbit 98

10 Fun with Bunny 106

part four

Beyond the Basics

11 Resources 120

Welcome

to the

World

of the

part one

External Features of the Rabbit

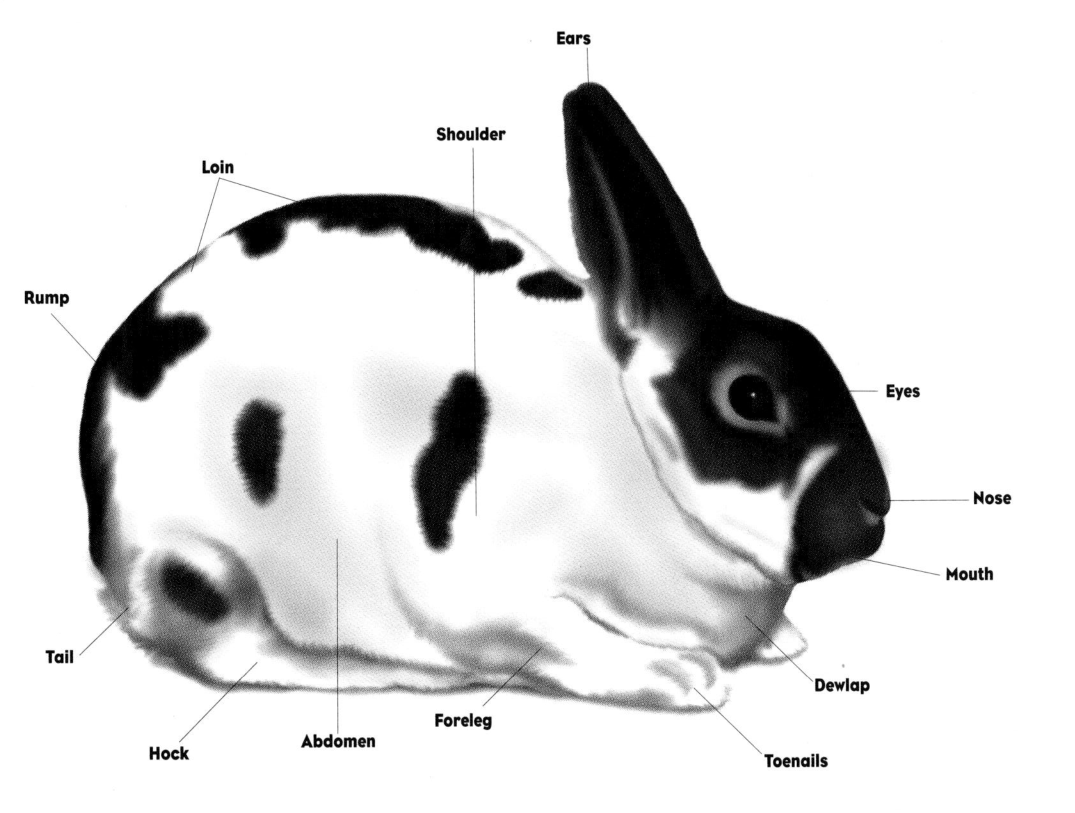

History

of the

Rabbit

Thousands of years ago, the rabbit was much like the adorable pet of today: its ears were long, its nose twitched incessantly, and it loved to groom its fur to perfection. But in other ways, the rabbit of antiquity and the rabbit of today are worlds apart.

The record of the rabbit's history begins with the earliest known rabbit fossils, which were found in China and Mongolia, and which date back nearly sixty-five million years to the Paleocene period. In North America, the oldest rabbit fossils are from the Oligocene period thirty-seven million years ago. These ancient species were the evolutionary forebears of today's wild rabbits; modern rabbits differ very little from today's fossil pictures of ancient rabbits.

Rabbits and Humans

The first signs of humankind's relationship with the rabbit appear in Spanish cave paintings dating from the Stone Age. Artists painted rabbits and hares, along with other animals, on the walls of caves during the Pleistocene period. During this time, the rabbit migrated down to southwestern Europe in an effort to escape the great cold of the Ice Age.

The descendants of the Ice Age rabbits were domesticated near the Mediterranean region in Europe and Africa around 600 B.C., when they were used for their meat and fur. They were traded extensively first by the Phoenicians and then later by other cultures, eventually spreading to America, Australia and New Zealand.

The rabbit's relationship with humans was not always as congenial as it is today.

Rabbit Overpopulation

Like most domesticated species in history, rabbits eventually escaped their captors or were deliberately set free, and soon populated the land. Because rabbits reproduce with such frequency, the natural predator/prey balance in these areas was upset; uncontrolled by natural enemies, rabbits were able to procreate with great rapidity. Feral rabbits were soon so great in number that they began to overgraze the land.

In the 1800s, feral rabbits in Australia multiplied to the point of overrunning the land. Crops were destroyed, and farmers waged a war on rabbits. Shooting, trapping and relentless hunting were practiced in an effort to rid the continent of an overabundance of rabbits.

Then, in the 1950s, biological warfare against rabbits was instituted. Scientists deliberately spread a virus called *myxomatosis* among feral rabbit populations in an effort to destroy them. This virus was initially successful and appeared to decimate the rabbit population. It later became evident, however, that some rabbits had developed a resistance to it. These immune rabbits eventually recolonized the areas, and the disease therefore had little long-term effect. Periodically, *myxomatosis* epidemics still recur in wild rabbit populations and sometimes among domestic rabbits, but the cycle of immunity repeats itself in the wild, and populations are restored.

The Rabbit Today

Until the Middle Ages, rabbits were considered a strictly agricultural commodity and were not raised as pets. However, during the fifth century, monasteries in France began keeping rabbits just for the enjoyment of creating different colored coats.

Rabbits have long been the subject of literature and other works or art.

In the 1700s, individuals began keeping rabbits as pets, and in the mid-1800s, rabbit owners who had originally used their animals only for food and fur started to develop specific breeds. Shortly thereafter, these owners began showing their rabbits at competitions. The hobby of showing and breeding rabbits developed unregulated until the mid-1930s when the British Rabbit Council was formed. The goal of the

council was to govern the fancy by supervising various rabbit clubs and registering rabbits throughout Great Britain.

The domestic rabbit population in the United States was probably first introduced by early explorers, although there is little written about the animal in America before the late 1800s. Rabbits were used primarily as food here until breeding and showing caught on late in the nineteenth century.

Once showing and breeding caught on as an activity in the early 1900s, the American Rabbit Breeders Association (ARBA) was founded to promote, encourage and develop the rabbit industry in the United States. ARBA is still the governing body for the rabbit fancy in this country. (See Chapter 10 for more on ARBA.)

RABBIT LORE

Throughout its history, the rabbit has had a notable affect on humankind. Aside from viewing the rabbit as a source of food and warmth, many cultures have also praised the rabbit for its swiftness and wit.

The most recognizable folktale involving a lagomorph is the story of the tortoise and the hare. Originally a fable from Africa, the story was later adopted and made famous by Aesop. The moral of the fable was designed to convince children that, regardless of how confident they are, they should not cut corners in life, as the hare did.

Native American peoples have revered the rabbit throughout history, and some tribes still view it as an important part of their culture. The Algonquins believe that the Great Hare rebuilt the world after an enormous flood, repopulating the world with his offspring. Consequently, according to the story, all humankind is related to the hare.

Rabbits vs. Hares

To the average person, there is not much difference between a rabbit and a hare. Scientifically they do have many things in common; both rabbits and hares belong to the order *Lagomorpha,* and the family, *Leporidae.* Since both are lagomorphs, they are similar in appearance. However, most people don't realize that there are considerable differences between rabbits and hares and that the two are actually classified as two different species.

The hare is generally the larger of the two, with longer legs and torso. While a rabbit's young are born hairless and with their eyes closed, baby hares have fur and are born with their eyes open. There are also considerable behavioral differences between the two species. Rabbits are highly sociable creatures and live underground in community groups when in the wild. Hares, on the other hand, are solitary creatures who prefer to live alone above ground. Because of this unsociable nature, hares are rarely appropriate as pets. In fact, unlike the rabbit, there is no domesticated species of hare. Some examples of wild hares are the Snowshoe hare, the Arctic hare and the jackrabbit (a misnomer). Wild rabbits include the cottontail, the brush rabbit and the European rabbit.

While rabbits and hares share much in common, they actually belong to two different species.

Rabbits, Hares and Rodents

Both the rabbit and the hare were once thought of as rodents because of their long front teeth. Scientists later discovered that while rabbits and hares share a common prehistoric ancestor with rodents, rabbits and hares are from a completely different order. The distinction between rodents and lagomorphs is small but noteworthy. While rodents have four front teeth, rabbits and hares have one more pair of incisors. Rabbits and hares also chew their food differently than rodents.

Bugs Bunny is America's most famous rabbit.

Rabbits in Popular Culture

The rabbit is a favorite subject in contemporary literature, particularly in fiction written for children. *The Tale of Peter Rabbit,* the story of a disobedient young bunny named Peter, has been read and loved by children around the world. The names of the characters in this book by Beatrix Potter have become synonymous with rabbits everywhere: Peter, Flopsy, Mopsy and Cottontail.

Another book about rabbits, *Watership Down,* by Richard Adams, has gained great notoriety, and deservedly so. Using natural rabbit behaviors to create a story about a group of rabbits trying to find a new home in the English countryside, Adams produced one of the most enjoyable animal stories ever written. *Watership Down* not only served to educate the public about rabbit behavior when it was published, but also stirred some sympathy for the plight of the rabbit in today's rapidly developing world.

Literature is not the only realm of popular culture in which rabbits are featured. One of the most famous rabbits of all is Bugs Bunny, the animated creation of Warner Brothers Studios. A staple in children's cartoons since the 1940s, Bugs Bunny continues to be a favorite personality among kids and the adults who grew up with him.

The widespread and widely noted presence of rabbits throughout history and throughout cultures is indicative of the many ways in which these curious and lovable animals enhance the lives of the humans who interact with them. The current increase in the number of households that keep rabbits as pets is the logical next chapter in the history of the rabbit.

MORE RABBIT LORE

The Iroquois tribe tells of a time when hunters came upon a large rabbit in a clearing. This rabbit turned out to be the chief of all rabbits. As the hunters stood by and watched, the Rabbit Chief summoned all his fellow rabbits and began a joyous dance. When the hunters returned to their village telling of what they had seen, a wise old woman explained to them that they had been shown a special dance meant to thank the rabbit for the food and warmth that it gave to them in the forms of its flesh and its fur. To this day, the Iroquois people still honor the rabbit with this very dance.

While Europeans believe that they see a man's face when they look up at the moon, some Eastern cultures see a rabbit, and believe this lunar creature to be the ruler of all the rabbits on Earth.

Of course, the Easter Bunny is probably the most famous legendary rabbit in our culture. In the German legend, a bird is turned into a rabbit by the Goddess of Spring. This bird-turned-rabbit continues to lay eggs, however. Thus, the popular Eastertime connection between bunnies and eggs.

chapter 2

Rabbits as Pets

Compared to a dog, a rabbit is a fairly easy pet to own. Rabbits don't need to go on long walks every day or to be taken to obedience school. The owner of a rabbit can leave his or her pet alone for several hours a day without having to worry about the need for bathroom breaks. On the other hand, rabbits are not maintenance-free pets

by any stretch of the imagination. They are social creatures who need a lot of love, attention and quality care.

The Right Pet for You?

To determine whether or not a rabbit would be a good pet for you, think about your lifestyle. Will your job, school or other commitments allow you to set aside time every day to spend with your rabbit?

Rabbits need daily interaction with other rabbits or with their owners to stay emotionally healthy. If you must leave a rabbit alone for many hours each day, you should probably have two rabbits, so they can keep each other company. Are you willing to make the commitment to spend several hours a day with your rabbit or to take on the responsibility of owning two of these creatures?

While sometimes seen as a fun and fleeting Easter gift, rabbits deserve a more serious commitment from their owners.

Rabbit Responsibilities

- Rabbits also need daily exercise. If your rabbit will be confined to a cage or hutch most of the time, will you be able to turn her out each day for supervised activity?
- You'll also need to scrub the cage every week or so, and you will have to clean out the soiled areas every day. In addition, you'll have to feed your pet and make sure she has fresh, clean water. Can you work these tasks into your schedule?
- Think about where you live. Do you have room to house a rabbit, either outside or inside your home? Is your neighborhood zoned for rabbits? Find out before you bring home a new pet.
- If you have children, are they old enough to learn how to handle the rabbit properly and treat her with respect?
- Do you have a dog or a cat? Before you add a rabbit to your household, you should think about how your other pets will react to the rabbit, and how this new addition to your family is going to affect them.
- If you intend to have your rabbit live in the house with you, then you must be willing to make changes in your environment. Rabbits are chewers, and homes that have rabbits must be rabbit-proofed.

- Another consideration is cost. The price of the rabbit and its cage is just the beginning. After you bring your pet home, you will have to pay for food, spaying or neutering and unlimited vet bills should your rabbit become ill.
- But most important of all, are you willing to make an emotional commitment to your rabbit? Are you prepared to accept responsibility for a living creature who is solely dependent on you for its well-being? Are you willing to make your pet's health and happiness a priority in your life? If your answer to these questions is yes, then you're ready to join the ranks of rabbit owners everywhere.

The Joys of Rabbit Ownership

Gaining Trust

In the world of pet ownership, there are few things more rewarding than knowing that a rabbit loves and trusts you. Your rabbit's love has to be earned, though, not bought. You can only establish this kind of rapport with your pet once you have spent time with her, showing her that you are worthy of her confidence. Gaining the trust of a rabbit can be difficult; rabbits are prey animals, and are therefore suspicious by nature. How else would they survive in the wild? They are often fearful and nervous, but once assured of their safety, the depths of their personalities come shining through.

Rabbit Intelligence

Intelligence is a quality often attributed to rabbits in popular legends, and rightly so. These bright creatures have complex social structures and develop relationships with individual people and even animals of other species. This high level of intelligence dictates that anyone living with a rabbit must stay on his or her toes. Rabbits are active, inquisitive and always exploring their environment. Because rabbits are good at figuring things out, they are notorious for opening doors, uncovering boxes and climbing into open drawers. Although endearing, this kind of behavior can get a rabbit into trouble. This is why you, as a rabbit owner, need to be especially vigilant about keeping track of your pet's whereabouts at all times.

Rabbits Can Be Trained

Many people find it surprising to know that rabbits can be taught their names. Rabbits can also learn to understand other words and can be trained to do a variety of tricks. Using a litter box and other behaviors can also be part of a well-trained rabbit's repertoire.

Rabbit Language

Like all animals, rabbits use body language to communicate with members of their own species. Humans who learn to understand this language will better understand what their companion rabbits are telling them on a daily basis. Being able to communicate with your rabbit as she communicates with you will only deepen the bond between you and your pet.

Rabbits and humans can learn to communicate through body language.

Rabbit owners soon discover that dogs and cats have not cornered the market when it comes to love and affection. Rabbits can be very warmhearted creatures and will even cuddle with and lick their favorite humans. They adore being petted and sometimes even enjoy napping in bed with a trusted person. Rabbits have been used in animal-facilitated therapy programs, helping patients overcome despondency and depression through regular visits. These animals have a huge capacity for affection and thrive when they receive love in return.

Finding a Rabbit

When it's time to embark on your journey to rabbit ownership, you'll want to start out on the right foot by looking for your new companion in the best way possible. You have several options from which to choose.

You may want to consider adopting a rabbit.

Adoption

If you are simply looking for a pet rabbit, you should first consider adoption. Just as with dogs and cats, there are homeless rabbits who need loving families. They deserve a second chance with a family who will love and care for them.

If you would like to adopt a rabbit, call the animal shelters in your area and inquire as to whether any rabbits are available for adoption. Since unwanted rabbits are euthanized at shelters just like dogs and cats, adopting a rabbit directly from a shelter means you will be saving a life.

You may also want to check the "pets" section of your local newspaper, as well as bulletin boards in supermarkets, veterinarians' offices and pet supply stores to see if there are people trying to find homes for rabbits in your area. Through a private individual, you may find a rabbit who is already litter box trained and spayed or neutered.

A group called the House Rabbit Society was formed in the 1980s to address the problem of unwanted rabbits and now works to rescue rabbits who are about to be destroyed in animal shelters. If you want to provide a rabbit with an indoor home and have been unable to find an adoptable rabbit in an animal shelter or through a private individual, the House Rabbit Society can refer you to a local chapter of its organization, who will then put you in touch with someone who has rabbits in need of new homes. (See Chapter 12 for information on how to contact this organization.)

HOW TO HOLD YOUR RABBIT

- Never pick a rabbit up by her ears.
- Slide one hand under the rabbit's front paws in the direction of her hind end.
- Place your other hand on the rabbit's rump.
- Lift the rabbit up, supporting the entire body with both hands.
- Hold the rabbit against your torso with her head facing the crook of your arm.
- Tuck the rabbit under your arm like a football and slide the hand underneath her body further toward her hindquarters to support her from head to tail along your forearm.
- Place your other hand on the rabbit's back to secure her.

Breeders

If you have seriously considered whether you want to own a rabbit, and you've decided to show your pet, purchasing is an important option. The best place to buy a rabbit is from a responsible breeder—a rabbit fancier who has researched bloodlines before breeding his or her rabbits, and who keeps his or her animals in a clean and healthy living environment. These breeders are experts on their breed of choice, and frequently show their animals. Once you have determined which breed you want, you can obtain the name and phone number of a breeder in your area by contacting the national club for each breed. (See

Chapter 12 for more information regarding these clubs.)

Your local 4-H group is another possible source for breeders. Call your local county extension office (listed in your telephone book) and ask for the name and number of a 4-H rabbit leader in your area. This person should be able to put you in touch with a breeder nearby.

Buying from a breeder offers an added bonus: Once you purchase your rabbit, you go home with the name and phone number of an experienced rabbit owner who can answer your questions and help you with your rabbit should you have any problems.

Age

Age is another factor to consider when buying a rabbit. While baby rabbits are adorable, they are also more fragile and harder to train. Adolescent rabbits (under one year) are known for being mischievous and sometimes difficult to handle. Adult rabbits, on the other hand, often make wonderful pets. Since rabbits live to be anywhere from six to ten years old, you can adopt or purchase a rabbit that is several years old, and still have a lot of time left to spend with your new friend.

If your heart is set on getting a baby rabbit, make sure the one you buy is at least eight weeks old. Taking young rabbits away from their mothers before the babies are two months of age can be both emotionally and physically damaging to the young rabbit. Prematurely removed rabbits rarely survive for long once they arrive in their new home.

Assessing Your Rabbit's Health

It's important to start out on the right foot by selecting a rabbit that is in good health. A rabbit's general health can be determined in a number of ways. Check to see if her ears and nose are clean and free of discharge and debris. Then, take a close look at her fur. The fur of a healthy rabbit will be soft, shiny and even.

Keep an eye out for ear and skin mites, bald spots and signs of diarrhea under the tail and in the rabbit's cage or litter box.

Feel the rabbit's body. Notice whether or not the rabbit feels too thin, and not round, tight and smooth. Check to see if its abdomen is hard and distended. A potbellied rabbit may be suffering from a worm infestation.

Buying a purebred rabbit will give you an idea of what to expect when she's grown.

The rabbit's mental state is also an important factor to take note of when determining her health. Look for an animal that is bright-eyed, alert and active. A rabbit who appears dull and listless is probably sick.

Look at the rabbit's teeth and determine whether or not the two top teeth overlap the two lower teeth. Unless you are prepared to have the teeth trimmed regularly by a veterinarian, do not buy a rabbit whose teeth do not fit together in this manner. A condition called *malocclusion,* where the upper incisors do not overlap the lower incisors, is a common and serious problem in rabbits. Because misaligned teeth do not wear down properly, they can grow out of control.

Be sure to take notice of the rabbit's surroundings. Are they clean and relatively odor-free? Are the animals kept in spacious, airy cages? Do the other rabbits appear healthy? Many rabbit diseases are contagious. If the rabbit you are considering for purchase is housed near a sick rabbit, chances are good that your rabbit will come down with the same illness.

Personality

If you give your rabbit love and attention, she will most likely become a wonderful pet. However, when you are selecting your rabbit, you may want to observe the personality of the animals you are considering to see which one strikes your fancy. Rabbits who appear nervous and afraid may be high strung, or simply not used to being handled. If the animal is young, it is still very impressionable and will learn to be held and stroked if you show it love and consideration. Older rabbits who have not been handled much will take more time before they feel comfortable with people. Eventually, however, they can become quite used to being touched and should learn to respond to care and affection.

A healthy rabbit will look bright-eyed and alert.

Male or Female

There is much debate in rabbit circles over which make better pets: males or females. The answer really depends on what you plan to do with your rabbit.

Does (females) are said to be territorial and aloof. Their main concern in life is reproducing. Breeding is so important to them that some females, when

not bred, will actually have false pregnancies. **Bucks** (males), on the other hand, are thought to be aggressive and unsettled. Much like male cats do, they also have the unpleasant tendency to mark their territory by spraying odorous urine.

A boy or a girl rabbit—neutered or spayed—will make a fine pet.

You can solve these problems in your rabbit of either sex quite simply: Have your rabbit spayed or neutered. Once this is done, their troublesome hormones will disappear, they will be healthier, and you will have a more gentle, loving pet. Preventing your pet from having a litter of kits will also help curb the rabbit overpopulation problem and reduce the number of rabbits put to sleep in animal shelters. Spaying and neutering will also eliminate the need to choose between getting a male or female pet; spayed females and neutered males make equally good pets.

Pedigrees

If you are purchasing a purebred rabbit from a breeder, ask the breeder for a signed pedigree paper. This document will state your rabbit's sex, color and parentage. You may later choose to register your rabbit with the American Rabbit Breeders Association if you want to show the animal at local rabbit shows. (See Chapter 12 for more information on showing.)

chapter 3

Rabbit Breeds

When the rabbit was first domesticated, there was only one "breed." Now, however, there are forty-five breeds of rabbits recognized by the American Rabbit Breeders Association. Obviously, this wide variety means that choosing one particular breed over another can be a daunting task.

Choosing a Breed

When determining which breed to acquire, keep your needs and lifestyle in mind. If you live in a small space and don't have room for a large cage, you may want to consider one of the dwarf breeds. If your time is limited, you'll definitely want to stay away from the

woolly breeds, since they require frequent grooming. If you have older children who plan to handle and maybe even show their rabbits, you'll want to stick to a smaller breed that they can easily lift.

Chocolate Mini Rex.

Taking these factors into account, narrow your choice down to several breeds, then find the one that appeals to you most.

In the next few pages, you'll find descriptions of the many coat and color varieties found among the different rabbit breeds. This information will help you better understand the actual breed descriptions that follow at the end of the chapter.

Coat Varieties

There are four different kinds of fur, or coats, on rabbits. **Normal rabbit fur** is the coat that most people imagine when they think about rabbits. It comes in two layers, an overcoat and undercoat. Both layers are approximately one inch in length. The undercoat is soft and insulates the rabbit against cold temperatures.

Rex fur is shorter than normal fur and is cottony and airy to the touch. It is much thicker than normal fur, and stands upright instead of laying flat against the rabbit's body. Rex fur also has a double coat.

The long and fluffy **Angora coat** is often used for spinning because of its warmth. Since it is used to make clothing, the Angora coat is often referred to as wool. The fur stands away from the rabbit's body, giving it a very fuzzy, hairy appearance.

Satin fur has fine, somewhat translucent hairshafts, that make it look silky and shiny. Satin coats are about the same length as normal fur coats, but are distinguishable by their luster.

Coat Color Patterns

As a whole, rabbit coats display an astounding number of colors and patterns, each with its own unique beauty. To make identification easier, these colors have been assigned to specific groups. A general definition of each group follows.

White and gray broken Mini Lop.

Agouti Pattern The hair-shaft on an agouti-colored rabbit has three or more bands of color, usually with a dark gray base. The head, feet and ears of an agouti-colored rabbit are usually ticked, while the circles around the eyes, the fur on the belly and the fur under the jaws tend to be lighter. This is the color pattern seen in wild rabbits. Agouti-colored rabbits come in chestnut, chocolate, sable, lilac and smoke pearl.

Brindle Pattern Brindle is an intermingling of two colors, one dark and one light. The brindle pattern appears consistently throughout the body.

Broken Pattern There are two different subdivisions within the broken pattern: bi-color and tri-color. A **bi-colored broken pattern** consists of any normal rabbit color in combination with white. For example, a bi-colored rabbit may be white with black spots. A **tri-colored rabbit,** on the other hand, will have two other colors in addition to white.

Marked Pattern Marked pattern rabbits are usually white, and have one other color that appears in a distinct pattern over the entire body.

Pointed White Pattern This type of rabbit is all white with a darker color on its nose, ears, feet and tail. These markings are much like those of a Siamese cat.

Self Pattern Rabbits whose coats consist of only one color solidly covering their entire bodies are said to carry a self pattern.

Shaded Pattern This pattern looks much like it sounds. Shaded rabbits show a gradual shift in color, beginning with a darker color on their backs, heads, necks, ears, legs and tails. The sides of these rabbits, however, are of a much more diluted shade of that same color.

Pointed White Jersey Wooly.

Solid Pattern This pattern is similar to the self pattern, except that it may include agouti and other mixed-color fur, as long as the colors do not create a pattern or a distinct marking.

Ticked Pattern This consists of a base color throughout the majority of the rabbit's fur, with the addition of contrasting solid or tipped guard hairs.

Wide Band Pattern Rabbits of this coloration have the same color on their bodies, heads, ears, tails and feet. Their eye circles, the underside of their tails, their jaws and stomachs have a lighter coloration.

Rabbit Colors

While each breed has its own breed standard and selection of color varieties, there are common colors that can be found in many different breeds. In addition to black and white, below are descriptions of some of the most common rabbit colors.

Beige Rabbits of this color have the pigment all over their bodies except on the napes of their necks, which is lighter. They have a bluish white color on their bellies and eye circles of the same color. Their eyes are brown with a ruby glow.

Blue The blue coloration can be described as a medium-shade of gray with a blue or lavender cast. The eyes of a blue-colored rabbit are blue-gray.

Castor A rich dark chestnut color, castor is sometimes also described as mahogany brown. Evenly distributed over the body, head and legs, castor fur is lightly tipped with black. The belly of a castor rabbit is white or tan, and its eyes are brown.

Castor Rex.

Chinchilla The standard chinchilla coloration consists of a blend of black and pearl with a dark gray base. Named after the coloring seen on actual chinchillas, rodents known for their lush fur, chinchilla rabbits also come in a chocolate version.

Chocolate A deep dark brown, this coloration features a light gray undercoat. The eyes are brown with a red cast in subdued light.

Fawn Fawn-colored rabbits have a deep golden color over their backs, flanks and chests. The eye circles, insides of ears, underjaws, tails and bellies are white. Fawn-colored rabbits have gray or brown eyes.

Lilac This coloration consists of a medium gray hue with a pinkish tint that is present over the rabbit's entire body. The eyes of these rabbits are the same color, and have a ruby glow in subdued light.

Lynx The body and the top of a lynx-colored rabbit's tail are tinged with lilac and light orange, and a sharper orange color shows through from underneath. There are white areas underneath the tail, belly and jaw. The eye circles and insides of the ears are also white; eyes are blue-gray.

Opal The hairshaft of an opal-colored rabbit features a pale blueish color on top with a fawn band below it. The eye circles and underside of the rabbit

are white with a dark gray undercoat. An opal's ears are laced with blue and its eyes are gray.

Siamese Siamese-colored rabbits look a lot like Siamese cats. They have dark brown color on their ears, head, feet, belly and tail, with a lighter body color distinct from the point colors. The eyes are brown.

Tortoiseshell Dutch.

Squirrel The hair-shaft on a rabbit with the squirrel coloration consists of a blend of gray and white bands. The color extends from the rabbit's back down along its sides, where it is met by white on the belly and on top of the hind feet. The nape of the neck, chest and eye circles are a lighter version of the original color. The upper part of the ears has a dark blue edge. The eyes are gray.

Steel This color configuration comes in black, blue, chocolate and lilac, as well as sable and smoke pearl colors. The entire body of the rabbit is covered with one of the above colors, the hairs of which are diffused with a small amount of gold or silver tipping, depending on whether the rabbit is a gold steel or a silver steel. The eyes are brown or gray.

Tan Pattern This coloration features a solid color on the head, back, sides, outside of ears, back legs, front of forelegs and top of the tail. A lighter color will appear on the eye circles, nostrils, jaw, chest and underside of the rabbit's body.

Tortoiseshell Rabbits with this coloration sport a lively orange on their bodies, which mingles into a grayish blue shadowing over the rump and haunches. The tail matches the orange color on top, and the color of the shadowing below. Tortoiseshell rabbits have brown eyes.

Popular Breeds

American The American rabbit, which has been in existence for nearly one hundred years, comes in two color varieties: blue and white. The blue variety has blue-gray eyes, while the white version has pink eyes. Compact in appearance, the American is a medium-size rabbit weighing around ten pounds. Its body has a mandolin shape; there is a slight arch over the loins and hindquarters and a taper from the hindquarters to the shoulders.

American Fuzzy Lop The Fuzzy Lop, originally created by crossbreeding the Holland Lop and the Angora, is available in a wide variety of colors. This variety of colors, along with the breed's furry coat and long, floppy ears, make the Fuzzy Lop very popular. This rabbit is shown in six different groups based on its color pattern: broken, pointed white, wide band, agouti, shaded and self. The agouti colors recognized for this breed are chestnut, chinchilla, opal and lynx. The broken colors of any recognized rabbit breed are allowed, as are solid blacks, whites, lilacs, blues and chocolates. A number of other color patterns are also found in this small rabbit, whose body is short and coupled. This cobby little rabbit's coat is long and woolly, and requires frequent grooming.

Broken Mini Lop.

American Sable This rabbit is well-named, since its coat, the result of several crosses with the chinchilla rabbit, is a beautiful dark brown. The ears, face, legs and tail of the American Sable are darker than the main part of its body. A medium-size rabbit with a slightly arched back, the American Sable weighs around nine pounds.

Angora There are four types of Angora rabbits: English Angora, French Angora, Satin Angora and Giant Angora. Each one is a separate breed and has the long, woolly hair typical of the Angora family. Angoras come in an astounding array of beautiful colors. Because of the Angora's dense coat, which grows to about three inches in length, the breed requires a good deal of grooming.

The **English Angora** comes in six color groups: the pointed white, self, agouti, shaded, wide band and ticked. Within these groups, the colors available are white with black; blue, lilac or chocolate points; solid blue, black, chestnut, agouti, chinchilla, chocolate agouti, chocolate chinchilla, copper, lilac, lilac chinchilla, lynx, squirrel, opal, wild gray, cream, red and fawn; shaded blue cream, chocolate tortoiseshell, dark sable, frosted pearl, lilac cream, smoke pearl, sable and tortoiseshell; and ticked chocolate steel, lilac steel, steel and blue steel. This breed, which originated in Turkey, is at least two hundred years old. Compact in size and stature, the English Angora weighs in at around six pounds.

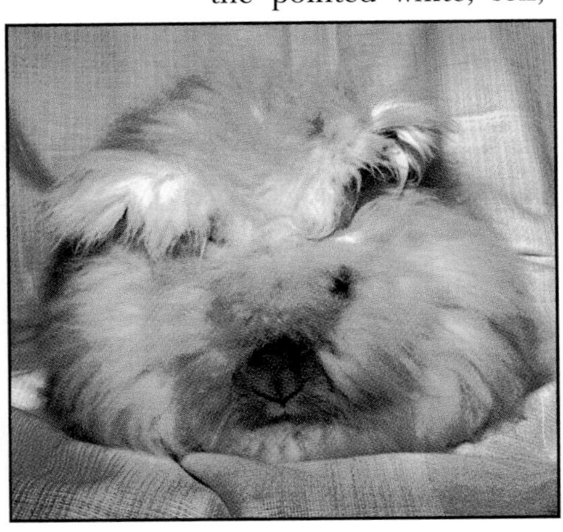

English Angora.

The **French Angora** comes in the same four color varieties as the English Angora, and in identical colors. While the two breeds are similar, the French Angora is somewhat bigger than the English, weighing in at around nine pounds. The French Angora also has less hair on its head, ears and legs. The French Angora, developed prior to the English Angora, was bred specifically for its wool. The French people used to hand pluck its wool and spin it for clothing.

The **Satin Angora** comes in the same color varieties as the English and French Angoras. The main difference between the Satin and the other Angoras is its coat.

The Satin, as its name implies, has shinier, silkier hair than its more wooly counterparts. Slightly smaller than the English Angora, Satins usually weigh around seven pounds.

Unlike the other Angora rabbit breeds, the **Giant Angora** is only available in white, with either blue or ruby eyes. It is larger than both the English and the Satin, weighing in at around nine pounds. Its coat is similar to the English Angora; it has especially long hair on its ears, face and legs (the hair on the legs is known as the furnishings).

White Self English Angora.

Belgian Hare Despite its name, the Belgian Hare is actually a domestic rabbit, not a hare. However, its long legs and ears do give it the appearance of a hare, hence its name. The breed was developed by Europeans in the late 1800s and was specifically bred for its lean, racehorse-like appearance. Only available in red chestnut, the Belgian Hare is a large-size rabbit of about nine pounds.

Beveren Not as frequently seen in the United States as some other breeds, the Beveren was developed in Europe and is colored either white, blue or black. A large rabbit weighing about ten pounds, the Beveren has a thick, silky coat. This rabbit is of medium length and has a slightly arched back.

Britannia Petite The tiny Britannia Petite is an all-white or black otter-colored rabbit that weighs only about two pounds. Known for being curious and alert, this rabbit can make a good pet for older children who will treat it gently. It is fine boned and light in stature.

Californian This very popular rabbit looks a lot like a Siamese cat, with its white coat and black-tipped ears,

nose, feet and tail. Somewhat large in size, the typical Californian weighs about nine pounds. Its body is plump and firm to the touch. Originally bred in the Golden State in the 1920s, this rabbit is related to and similar in appearance to the Himalayan.

Champagne D'Argent The coat of this rabbit contains a marvelous mixture of colored hairs, resulting in a wonderful silver-looking effect. This rabbit, a very old breed, was originally bred for its fur in the Champagne province of France. The D'Argent is medium in size, weighs about ten pounds, and is a popular pet in the United States.

Broken Mini Rex.

Checkered Giant The Checkered Giant comes in black and blue color varieties. The breed is typically white with dark markings, including a "butterfly" on the nose, dark ears, dark circles around the eyes, spots on the cheeks and various other dark patches on the body. Weighing a solid eleven pounds or more, the Checkered Giant is related to the Flemish Giant. It was first brought to America from Europe in 1910 and has a long, well-arched body.

Chinchilla There are three types of Chinchilla rabbit: Standard, American and Giant. All three types have the coloring of an actual chinchilla and are popular pets because of their attractive coats.

The **Standard Chinchilla** is the foundation of the Chinchilla breed and weighs around six pounds. Reportedly developed in France by crossbreeding a wild gray rabbit with some domestic strains of the species, the breed was first shown in 1913. It has a medium body with a slight arch to the back.

The **American Chinchilla** is the middle-weight of the three Chinchilla breeds, coming in at around ten pounds. It was bred down from the Standard variety for its size.

The largest Chinchilla, the **Giant,** is the result of a crossbreeding of the Flemish Giant with a smaller Chinchilla, orchestrated by an American breeder sometime after World War I. It was originally developed to be a meat rabbit, but makes a nice, albeit large, pet at about fourteen pounds.

Chestnut Agouti Netherland Dwarf.

Cinnamon This breed comes only in the reddish color indicative of its name. The ears, face and feet bear a darker shade of this same color. Occasional shades of gray on various parts of its body contribute to this breed's unusual appearance. Cinnamons, which are related to the New Zealand White, the Checkered Giant, the Californian and the Chinchilla, weigh approximately ten pounds.

Creme D'Argent The Creme D'Argent, which originated in France, is a handsome rabbit with an exquisitely colored coat of pale orange. Lighter guard hairs give this rabbit a smooth and silky appearance. Typically, the Creme D'Argent weighs about nine pounds.

Dutch The Dutch is an extremely popular rabbit, and is easily recognizable because of its markings. Available in six color varieties, the Dutch has a dark head with a white nose and blaze, and dark "britches." Its dark eyes blend into the color on its face, which can

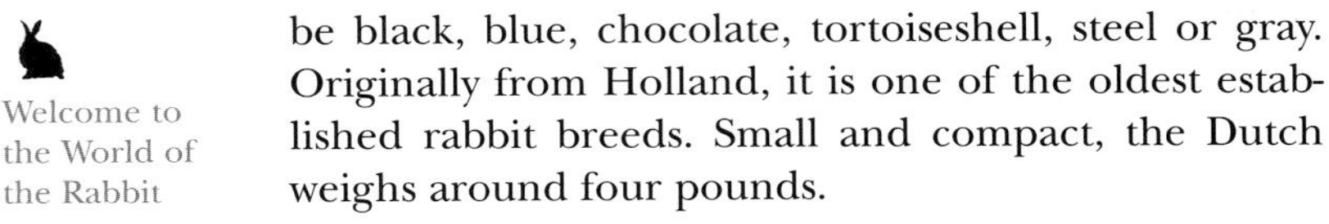

be black, blue, chocolate, tortoiseshell, steel or gray. Originally from Holland, it is one of the oldest established rabbit breeds. Small and compact, the Dutch weighs around four pounds.

Dwarf Hotot At first sight, the tiny Dwarf Hotot appears to be wearing eyeliner! The breed's characteristic black eyebands certainly give it this look. Only seen in white with dark eyes, the Dwarf Hotot weighs about three pounds and was bred down from the Hotot in the 1970s.

Pointed White Mini Lop.

English Spot The English Spot, or English for short, is reminiscent of a Dalmatian with its white coat and dark spots. The breed comes in seven different color varieties, of which the breed's markings are made: black, blue, chocolate, gold, gray, lilac and tortoiseshell. A capped nose, dark ears, eye rings and a stripe along the back are all characteristic of this breed, which weighs about eight pounds. A very old breed whose popularity began in England in the late 1800s.

Flemish Giant Massive in size, the Flemish Giant is the largest breed of rabbit and weighs over fourteen pounds. Available in steel gray, light gray, black, blue, white, sandy and fawn, this breed is very popular as a pet despite its large size. Seen quite often at rabbit shows, the Flemish Giant originated in Belgium.

Florida White This breed of rabbit is the one most commonly used for laboratory research. Developed by crossing the Dutch, Polish and New Zealand White, the breed is relatively new, having been accepted by the American Rabbit Breeders Association in the early 1960s. The Florida White comes in white only, as its name implies, and has pink eyes. It weighs about five pounds.

Harlequin The Harlequin, an interesting, medium-size and unusually marked rabbit of about eight pounds, was developed in France in the 1800s. Available in two color groups and four actual colors, the Harlequin's coat is best described as having an "ice-cream sundae" look. Different colors swirl and blend in unique configurations on the coat. The base coloring of a **Japanese Harlequin** alternates with strips of orange or a lighter version of the base color. The **Magpie Harlequin**'s base coloring alternates with strips of white. The heads of Harlequin rabbits are split in half by color; each rabbit can look like two different ones when viewed from one side and then the other! Harlequin base colors are black, blue, lilac and chocolate.

Havana The small, shiny Havana was created from a single rabbit born to an unpedigreed doe in Holland in 1898. While it first appeared in chocolate, the Havana is now available in blue and black varieties as well. Prized for its coat, the Havana is short and compact, weighing about six pounds.

Broken Castor Mini Rex.

Himalayan The Himalayan breed has been around for many years, reportedly originating near the Himalayan Mountains. More widely distributed around the world than any other breed of rabbit, it is very popular in China and Russia, as well as in the United States. Distinctive because of its white coat and blue or black markings, this rabbit is small in size and usually weighs only four pounds.

Hotot In France, this breed is known as the Blanc de Hotot, or the "white of Hotot," Hotot being the area where it was developed. The breed was first imported into the United States in the late 1970s. Available only in a frosty white color with thin black eye circles, the

Hotot is a medium-size rabbit weighing around nine pounds.

Jersey Wooly A recently developed breed of rabbit created in the 1970s through crossbreeding, the Jersey Wooly was created specifically for its luxurious coat. The fur of the Jersey Wooly is available in the agouti (chestnut, chinchilla, opal, squirrel), pointed white (black or blue markings), self (black, blue, chocolate, lilac, blue-eyed white, ruby-eyed white), shaded (sable point, seal, Siamese sable, smoke pearl, tortoiseshell, blue tortoiseshell) and tan pattern (black otter, blue otter, silver marten, sable marten, smoke pearl marten) color groups.

A small rabbit, the Jersey Wooly weighs about three pounds. This breed is known for its gentle temperament and for being an exceptional pet. However, because of its long coat, the Jersey Wooly does require regular grooming.

Lilac The Lilac comes in one color, a light pinkish gray. Originally considered an anomaly, the Lilac began as a result of an unusual coloration within the Havana breed. Weighing about seven pounds, the body of the Lilac is substantial and compact.

Lop The Lop rabbits are probably the most distinctive and easily recognizable of all the breeds. Lop breeds of the past included rabbits whose ears flopped forward over their faces and rabbits whose ears both flopped over to the same side. These breeds are extinct now, and the Lop we see today is the Lop of choice.

The modern Lop has huge ears, which flop down beside its head like a hound dog's, and give it the special look unique to the breed. Along with those big ears comes a wonderful personality. Since Lops were bred specifically for show and pet purposes, they tend to be very people oriented. Owners of Lops report that they are amusing rabbits to live with, and are affectionate and sensitive. However, because their ears hang down instead of standing straight up, the Lop is prone to more ear infections than other breeds.

There are four breeds of Lop rabbits: the English Lop, French Lop, Holland Lop and Mini Lop. Each breed is unique in both its appearance and history.

The **English Lop** is one of the oldest breeds of domestic rabbit still in existence. Developed at least as early as the 1800s, the English Lop was the first of the lop-eared breeds. Weighing in at approximately ten pounds, the English Lop comes in broken and solid color patterns. Within those patterns, many of the typical rabbit colors are found. When being judged at rabbit shows, the ears are the most important aspect of this well-balanced breed. The ears of an adult English Lop measure twenty-five inches or more in length.

The **French Lop** was first developed in France in the 1800s out of a breeding between the English Lop and the Flemish Giant. The French Lop differs from the English in that it is characterized by a heavier stature and shorter ears. The French Lop weighs in at around ten pounds and comes in two color varieties: solid and broken. It can be found in many different rabbit colors.

Black Silver Marten, Red-eyed White and Siamese Sable Netherland Dwarfs.

The **Holland Lop,** a dwarf breed of Lop, was created in Holland in the 1960s. It displays the same color varieties as the French and English: agouti, broken, pointed white, self, solid, shaded and ticked. Holland Lops are available in any recognized rabbit color. Also known as the Netherland Dwarf Lop, the tiny, compact Holland Lop weighs only about four pounds.

The **Mini Lop** is also a relatively new breed of Lop. Developed during the 1970s in Germany, the Mini Lop was originally called the Klein Widder until its name was changed in the 1980s when it was recognized by the American Rabbit Breeders Association. The Mini

Lop is similar to the French Lop, but its mere five-pound weight makes it significantly smaller. The breed comes in the usual Lop color varieties of agouti, broken, pointed white, self, shaded, solid and ticked. All recognized rabbit colors can be seen in the Mini Lop.

Mini Rex The Mini Rex was developed using the standard-sized Rex. This breed is growing in popularity as a pet and show rabbit because of its luxurious fur and small size. Weighing about four pounds, this breed is available in the same color varieties and colors as its larger cousin, the Rex.

Broken Copper Satin.

Netherland Dwarf The very popular Netherland Dwarf is the smallest of all domestic rabbits, weighing no more than two pounds. Its tiny stature, wide range of colors, small ears and large eyes make it a very popular pet. Part of its appeal is no doubt the result of its baby-like features; fully grown adult Netherland Dwarfs still resemble kits (baby rabbits). The Netherland Dwarf comes in the following color varieties and colors: self (white with ruby eyes, white with blue eyes, black, blue, chocolate, lilac); shaded (Siamese sable, Siamese smoke pearl, sable point); agouti (chinchilla, lynx, opal, squirrel, chestnut); tan (sable marten, silver marten, smoke pearl marten, otter, tan); and any other variety (fawn, Himalayan, orange, steel, tortoiseshell).

New Zealand The New Zealand comes in three distinct color varieties: white, black and red. The red was the first color to appear after what experts believe was a cross between a Belgian Hare and a white rabbit. Despite what its name implies, this breed, created for meat, fur and research purposes, was developed in the United States. The New Zealand has not been confined to its original function, however, and has become a popular pet and show rabbit. Typical New Zealands weigh about ten pounds.

Palomino A relatively new breed, the Palomino was developed in the United States and comes in two color varieties: golden and lynx. The golden color is similar to the coat colors seen in the Palomino horse, hence the breed's name. Weighing about nine pounds, the Palomino has a slightly arched back.

Polish A tiny rabbit weighing only about three pounds, the Polish is believed to have developed in England in the 1800s. Commonly seen at rabbit shows, this breed comes in five different color varieties: blue, black, chocolate, blue-eyed white and ruby-eyed white. Some experts believe that the name does not refer to the country of Poland, but rather to its shiny coat.

Rex The fur of the Rex rabbit looks and feels like plush velvet. This breed, which comes in a wide variety of colors, is very popular as a pet and show rabbit. Created in 1919 from a mutation, the Rex's unusual coat can be attributed to its lack of longer guard hairs. Weighing approximately nine pounds, the Rex comes in black,

BREEDS RECOGNIZED BY THE AMERICAN RABBIT BREEDERS ASSOCIATION

American	Harlequin
American Fuzzy Lop	Havana
American Sable	Himalayan
Angora, English	Hotot
Angora, French	Jersey Woolly
Angora, Giant	Lilac
Angora, Satin	Lop, English
Belgian Hare	Lop, French
Beveren	Lop, Holland
Californian	Lop, Mini
Champagne D'Argent	Mini Rex
Checkered Giant	Netherland Dwarf
Chinchilla, American	New Zealand
Chinchilla, Giant	Palomino
Chinchilla, Standard	Polish
Cinnamon	Rex
Creme D'Argent	Rhinelander
Dutch	Satin
Dwarf Hotot	Silver
English Spot	Silver Fox
Flemish Giant	Silver Marten
Florida White	Tan

black otter, blue, Californian, castor, chinchilla, chocolate, lilac, lynx, opal, red, sable, seal, white and broken group varieties. All known rabbit colors are seen in the Rex.

Rhinelander The Rhinelander has an unusual coloration that can best be described as patches of calico, much like those that appear on a calico cat. The breed's base color is white, and its nose, ears, cheeks, eyes, back and sides are marked with black and orange. Developed in Europe, the Rhinelander is a medium- to large-size rabbit weighing anywhere from seven to ten pounds.

Seal Rex.

Satin The Satin is so named because of its soft, shiny coat. Created in the United States from a mutation within the Havana breed, the Satin comes in ten different color groups: black, blue, Californian, chinchilla, chocolate, copper, red, Siamese, white and broken. The Satin is a medium-size rabbit that weighs about nine pounds.

Silver The Silver got its name from its coat's unique coloring, a silvery sheen created by a mixture of white hairs against a dark background. Believed to have originated in India centuries ago, the Silver breed was refined in England during the height of rabbit show popularity. Available in black, brown and fawn, Silvers weigh anywhere from four to seven pounds.

Silver Fox Originally bred in Europe for its fur, the Silver Fox has an unusual coat. Measuring an inch or more in length with a thick undercoat, the fur of the Silver Fox comes in black or blue varieties. Once called the American Heavyweight Silver, this breed is on the large size, weighing about ten pounds.

Silver Marten Created using the Chinchilla rabbit, the Silver Marten has guard hairs that are gray-tipped on a dark background of black, blue, chocolate or sable. The areas around the eyes and nose are also gray. Silver Martens typically weigh about eight pounds.

Tan The color and markings of the Tan are reminiscent of a Doberman Pinscher, particularly the black and chocolate varieties. The top part of the body is dark, while the underside is tan. The tan coloring also appears around the eyes and nose, under the neck and inside the rims of the ears. Supposedly the result of an accidental mating between a wild buck and a Dutch doe in England during the 1800s, the breed has been popular for decades. The Tan is a small- to medium-size rabbit, weighing approximately five pounds.

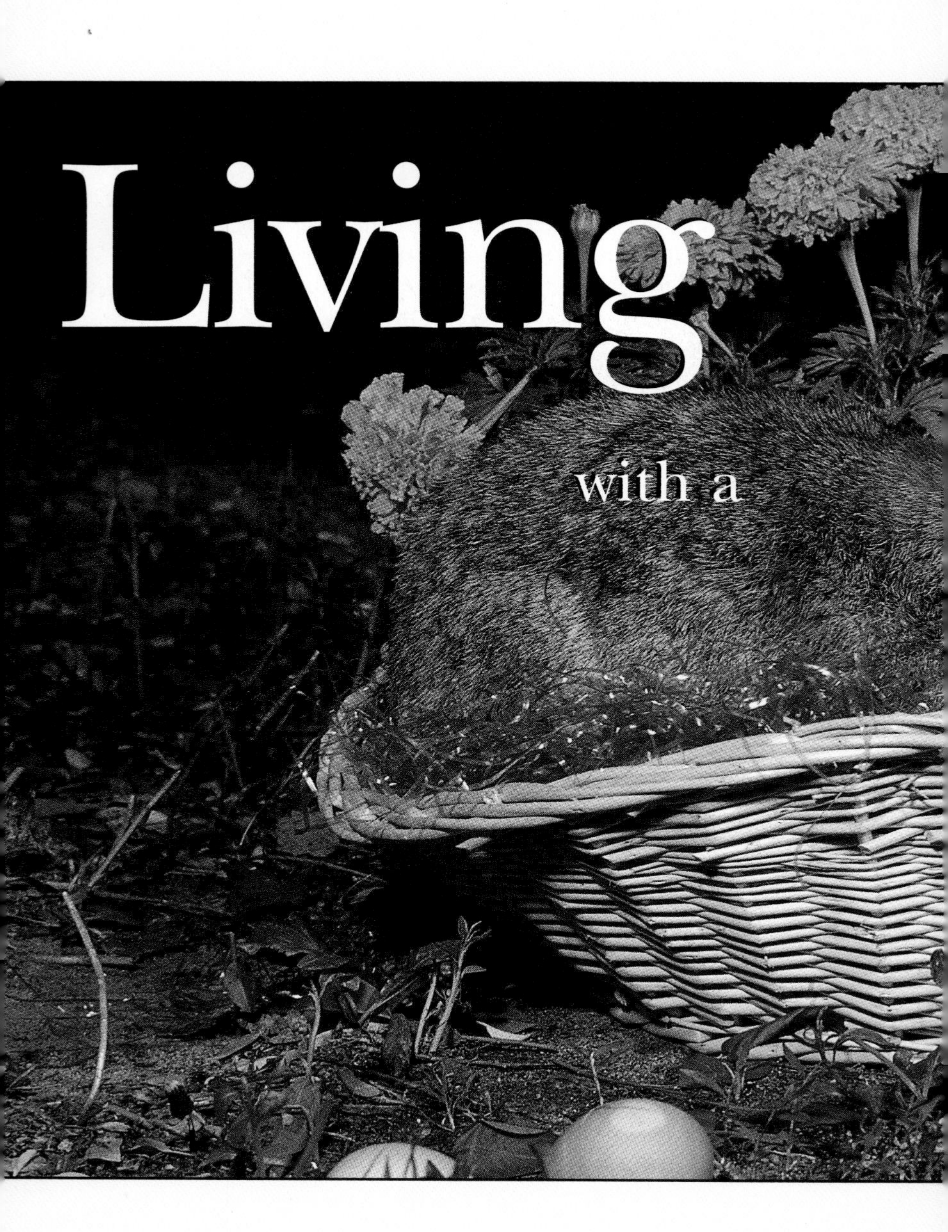

Living

with a

part two

Rabbit

chapter 4

Bringing Bunny Home

You've chosen the rabbit that you are going to adopt or purchase. Before you bring him home, you will need to prepare his environment. Shopping for and setting up all the equipment and supplies you'll need for your rabbit in advance of his arrival will make his introduction to your home less stressful for both of you.

What You'll Need

The first and most important item to purchase is your rabbit's **hutch** or **cage.** If you are buying an outdoor hutch, this will be your most significant financial investment. Take your time finding the one that best suits your needs. You can also consider building it yourself. If you decide on this option, leave yourself plenty of time to construct it before its inhabitant arrives. (See page 67 for information on how to buy a hutch, and page 58 for information on how to buy an indoor cage.)

You should also purchase or create a **nestbox** for your rabbit. This will help him feel more secure. (See page 60 for information on nestboxes.)

Cage Amenities

Your rabbit will need more than just a cage to live a comfortable and healthy life. There are a number of cage accessories that you should purchase before his arrival.

Food Dishes

Your rabbit's food bowl is very important and should be chosen wisely. Don't use just any old dish you have in the cupboard, since rabbits will chew up or knock over the wrong kind of food container. Instead, take a trip to your local pet supply store and buy a ceramic crock made specifically for pets. Ceramic crocks are difficult to knock over and are chew-resistant.

The size of the crock you should buy will depend on the size of your rabbit. Don't buy a dish that's too small for a large rabbit to put his head into, or one that's too big for a small rabbit to reach into comfortably.

Another option for a food dish is a metal bowl that attaches to the side of the cage. Make sure that the bowl you select is shallow enough to allow the rabbit to reach all the way into it. Attach the bowl low enough on the side of the cage for the rabbit to eat from it easily.

Water Bottles

Another necessity for your rabbit's cage is a water bottle. Gravity water bottles are readily available in pet supply stores. These are the best type of water containers for rabbits since they are impossible to knock over and they keep the water clean by preventing food or other matter from getting into it.

When you purchase a water bottle for your rabbit's cage, make sure it's not too small. You want your rabbit to drink as much water as possible to maintain his health. The only way to ensure that this happens is to make sure the water bottle is always full. It's simply easiest to have a larger bottle, especially if you are away from home for most of the day; an inadequately sized bottle will need filling more than once a day.

Using a hay rack inside your rabbit's cage will help keep both the hay and the cage cleaner.

Also, make sure the water bottle you purchase has a metal ball inserted into the tip. This will prevent the water from leaking into your rabbit's cage.

Hay Rack

A hay rack is another important item for your rabbit's cage. Hay is a vital element in your rabbit's daily diet. A hay rack will hold the hay in place so it doesn't get scattered throughout your rabbit's cage. Hay racks are usually made of metal and are constructed to attach to the top side of the cage. The rabbit can pull strands of hay from the rack whenever he gets the urge to munch.

Bedding

You'll want to have bedding on hand for your rabbit as well. Rabbits enjoy sleeping on straw or wood shavings. Straw can be obtained from a feed store, while wood shavings made especially for small animals can be purchased in any pet supply shop. If you use straw or wood shavings, don't be alarmed if your rabbit nibbles on his bedding. You can also use a blanket for your rabbit's bedding. Some rabbits love to lay on or under blankets. Just be sure that your rabbit doesn't chew on the blanket, since swallowing cloth fibers is dangerous to his health.

Chewing Blocks

Since rabbits are gnawing mammals, you should provide your rabbit with something safe and chewable to satisfy his munching instincts. The best things to use are chewing blocks. Untreated wood is satisfactory, but the safest items are commercially prepared wood blocks or chews, available in pet supply stores. Offered in a variety of colors and shapes, these safe and inexpensive gnawing treats are made especially for this purpose.

Toys

Many people are surprised to learn that rabbits love to play with toys. A toy for a rabbit can be anything from an empty toilet paper roll to a commercially made cat toy complete with squeaker. Having a few items on hand when your rabbit arrives will help him feel at home in his new environment. While he might not play with these items right away, once he becomes acclimated to his new environment, he will appreciate their presence.

Your rabbit will appreciate having a few toys on hand to play with.

Other Items

Besides the above-mentioned cage accessories, there are a few other articles you'll want to have on hand before you bring your rabbit home.

Travel Carrier

First and foremost is a travel carrier. You should purchase one before your rabbit makes the trip home with you, since you may need to use it for that journey.

Special carriers are made just for rabbits, but these are used primarily for show rabbits and are hard to find. If you can't find a rabbit carrier, opt for a traditional cat carrier instead. Make sure you line the carrier bottom with newspaper so the rabbit won't slide around during the car ride home. This carrier will also come in handy for trips to the vet and for confining your rabbit whenever you clean his cage or need to keep him temporarily in a small space. A good carrier is a wise investment.

Grooming Supplies

Since rabbits need regular grooming, a brush or comb should be on your shopping list. A slicker or pin brush is best for brushing rabbit fur. This type of brush is gentle yet effective at removing snarls and mats.

Believe it or not, it is possible to walk a rabbit on a leash; consider getting one as part of your set-up supplies.

If your rabbit is a shorthaired breed, then a flea comb (the type used for cats) will be the best tool for combing him. If your rabbit is of a longhaired variety, then you'll need a wide-toothed comb rather than a fine-toothed flea comb.

Since a rabbit's toenails need to be trimmed on a regular basis, make sure to have a nail trimmer on hand. The guillotine type used for cutting cats' nails will work, although many rabbit owners prefer to use human nail clippers instead.

Harness and Leash

If you someday want to train your rabbit to walk on a harness, consider purchasing a small adjustable cat harness at a pet supply store when you buy your other rabbit items. Rabbits can learn to walk on a leash much in the same way cats do. (See Chapter 10 for more information about harness training.)

Food

A supply of food (not more than one month's worth) should be on hand. Find out what your rabbit has been eating in his previous home and begin by offering him these same items. If you need to change his diet, you'll have to do so gradually over a period of a few weeks so as not to upset his digestion. (See Chapter 7 for information on what to feed your rabbit.)

Litter Box

A litter box is another necessity if you are planning to litter box train your rabbit. A litter box made for a cat can be good for use with a rabbit, providing the box is not too large. A giant-size breed will do fine with a standard-size kitty litter box, but a dwarf or small breed rabbit will need a smaller box. (See Chapter 5 for information on what types of litter to buy and how to go about litter box training your rabbit.)

Getting Your Newcomer Acclimated

When your new rabbit comes into your home for the first time, it will be an exciting moment. Everyone in the family will be anxious to touch his soft fur and watch him investigate his new environment.

As exhilarating as this moment will be, it is important to realize that your rabbit will have a different perspective on the situation. Put yourself in his place for a moment: He's just been taken from his familiar surroundings, stuck in a box and whisked away to a new place that he's never seen. Everything is new to him. There's little doubt that he will be feeling rather overwhelmed.

Because of the rabbit's built-in need to always be on the alert for predators, you may notice that your new pet seems skittish and fearful in his new environment.

Remember that this is normal rabbit behavior. Your pet will need a lot of love, patience and understanding to learn to relax. Be sure to give him a place to hide while he is being introduced to his new situation. This will provide him with much-needed security.

HOUSING DO'S AND DON'TS

- Clean your rabbit's cage or hutch regularly.
- If you provide a blanket for your rabbit's bedding, check to make sure he's not chewing on it.
- If your hutch is wooden, make sure the interior is covered with wire to prevent your rabbit from gnawing on the wood.
- Don't place the cage or hutch in an area of excessive heat or cold.
- Keep the hutch or cage away from drafts.
- Make sure the cage or hutch is free of sharp edges and corners.
- Rabbit-proof the interior of your home if you plan to have your rabbit indoors; remove exposed wires, cords, and dangerous chemicals.
- Make sure the cage or hutch is large enough to house the rabbit's necessities and still provide enough room for the rabbit to move around in freely.
- Don't place the cage or hutch in an area of continuous or excessive activity or noise.

The kindest way to let your rabbit get used to his new home is to leave him alone for a while. Place him in his cage, which will be equipped with food, water and everything he'll need to survive, and then just let him check things out in privacy for a couple of hours. After your rabbit has had a chance to get used to his new cage, you can then begin to quietly observe him. Speak to him softly every so often to reassure him that everything is okay and let him get accustomed to your voice.

Kids and Rabbits

If you have children, this is a good time to start teaching them how to treat their new rabbit. Explain to them that their new pet needs peace and quiet so he can learn to feel comfortable in his new home. Be sure that your children understand that they should not handle the rabbit right away. Because the new rabbit will be fearful and skittish, any attempts to hold him may result in injury to both child and rabbit. It's vital that you first learn the proper way to handle a rabbit, teach your children to emulate your behavior and then supervise the children while they handle the rabbit. (See pages 16 and 49 for instructions on how to properly handle your rabbit.) It is not recommended that very small children (under eight years old) be permitted to pick up or carry a rabbit. Petting a rabbit while it has all four feet safely on the floor is a better approach when very young children are involved.

If your children are anxious to show their new rabbit to their friends, ask their friends to come in to visit one or two at a time so they don't scare the animal. They should be as quiet as possible when they are near the new rabbit, since rabbits' ears are very sensitive; loud noises can frighten them.

Handling Your Rabbit

Rabbits do not like to be lifted and held unless they are gradually taught to tolerate it. If your rabbit has not been held very much in his life, it will require skill and patience to teach him to accept being held.

The most important thing to remember when holding your rabbit is to support both his upper and lower body equally.

Since rabbits are not natural climbers, your pet will feel awkward and insecure when lifted off the ground. As a result, he will struggle frantically or kick out violently. A fall can seriously injure a rabbit and so can violent kicking, which may result in a broken back. It is for these reasons that you must learn to hold your rabbit properly and securely. (Before you begin practicing picking up and carrying your rabbit, be sure to wear protective clothing. Bare skin and rabbit nails don't mix!)

The first rule of handling a rabbit is to never lift a rabbit by his ears. This practice is dangerous and painful for the rabbit and is inhumane.

There are several correct ways to hold a rabbit, depending on the size of the rabbit and how comfortable the animal feels when being held. One common

method is to slide one hand underneath the rabbit's chest between his front paws, with your fingers facing the hind end. Place your other hand on the rabbit's rump. Lift the rabbit with the hand under the chest while supporting the hind end with your other hand. Hold the rabbit against your torso with his head facing the crook of your elbow. Tuck the rabbit under your arm as if he were a football. Then slide your hand under his chest along his underside until your hand is supporting his hindquarters. Place your other hand on the rabbit's back to secure him. This is a good carrying position that feels safe to the rabbit.

Another method that works with smaller rabbits is to take hold of the animal's scruff (the loose skin on the back of the neck) with one hand, and place your other hand under his rump. As you begin to lift the rabbit by the scruff, support the weight of its hind end with your other hand. Bring the rabbit close to your body right away to provide him with security. (This method only works well for rabbits who don't kick when they are held.)

Remember when handling your rabbit to always treat him gently and carefully. Since being lifted and carried are not natural rabbit experiences, you will need patience and kindness to help your new rabbit accept this type of handling.

Introducing Other Pets

Rabbits are very sociable animals. In the wild, they live in large groups and have a complex social hierarchy. They therefore can get along very well with other pets, including cats, dogs and other rabbits. However, whether or not there is harmony in a particular multipet household depends largely on the individual animals involved, as well as the owner.

If your rabbit is going to live in your house and have the opportunity to move about freely, he will need to get along with your other pets. It can take considerable time, patience and commitment to teach your dog or cat to get along with a new rabbit. Never force pets on each other and always supervise your animals until you are completely convinced that you can trust them alone together.

Dogs

When it comes to dogs, rabbit owners have to take special care. Dogs and rabbits are natural enemies; dogs are predators and rabbits are prey animals. It is instinctive for dogs to chase and even kill rabbits, and it's instinctive for rabbits to fear dogs and run from them. If you are going to keep both a rabbit and a dog as pets, you need to be aware of this inherent tension between the two creatures.

After taking a few weeks to settle in, your rabbit will be ready to join the family!

If you already have a dog and would like to bring a rabbit into your home, there are some points you should consider. First of all, think about your dog's personality. Is she a mellow old coach potato who is hard-pressed to get upset or excited? Or is she a younger, more active dog? Dogs who are older and calmer usually do better when new pets are introduced. A quiet, elderly dog is less likely to chase a rabbit.

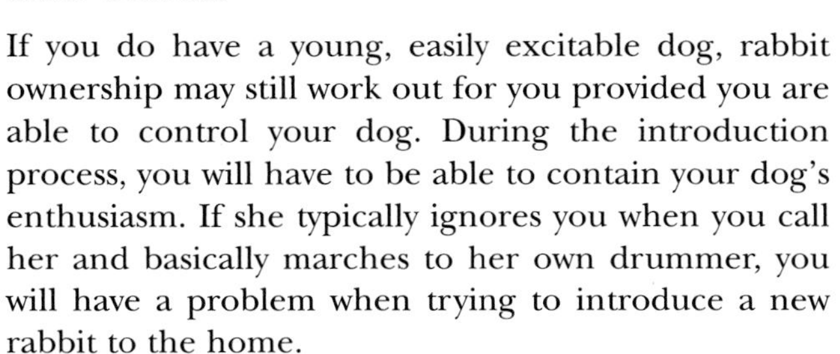

If you do have a young, easily excitable dog, rabbit ownership may still work out for you provided you are able to control your dog. During the introduction process, you will have to be able to contain your dog's enthusiasm. If she typically ignores you when you call her and basically marches to her own drummer, you will have a problem when trying to introduce a new rabbit to the home.

Assuming that your dog is controllable, think about her past relationships with other animals. Is she aggressive toward cats? Does she like to chase rabbits when you take her camping? Does she receive

encouragement to do this? If your answer to these questions is yes, you will have a difficult time teaching your dog that the new rabbit is hands-off, since she has already spent considerable time learning that it's okay to chase smaller animals. You can certainly give it a try, but you may have to consider keeping the two animals apart indefinitely or simply passing on rabbit ownership.

If you have determined that your dog is controlled enough to attempt making friends with a rabbit, you can begin the gradual process of introducing the two animals. Start the proceedings by placing your dog on a leash and asking an adult whom the dog respects to be in control of the other end.

While dogs and rabbits are natural enemies, there are instances in which the two can become friends.

Allow your dog to gradually approach the rabbit's cage in a quiet manner. If the dog gets rambunctious, correct her by boldly saying "no" and quickly jerking the leash. When the dog approaches quietly, praise her to let her know that this is the kind of behavior you expect when she is close to the rabbit.

When your rabbit first lays eyes on your dog, he will undoubtedly be frightened. He will probably dive into his nestbox and hide. Let him stay there, since he will feel much more secure this way. Eventually, if the dog behaves in a nonthreatening manner, the rabbit will become braver and more curious, finally venturing out of the nestbox to investigate.

Once the dog and rabbit are comfortable with each other in this scenario, and once your rabbit is comfortable being out of his cage without the dog being present, you can try allowing them to come face-to-face without the cage. Begin by placing the dog on a leash. You may also want to muzzle her, just to be safe.

Take your rabbit out of the cage and place him on a sofa or chair where he will be off the ground. (Don't place him too high just in case he jumps off.) Stay next to the rabbit and reassure him with stroking and a soothing voice while the person holding the leash allows the dog to slowly approach. If the dog acts aggressively, correct her by saying "no" and jerking on the leash. If she nears the rabbit quietly to sniff him, praise her.

The rabbit, frightened by the dog's proximity and by being outside of his cage, may dart away. Your dog's first impulse will be to chase him. Teach the dog that this is not acceptable. Using her obedience training, tell her to "sit" or "down" so that she will come to understand that this is a "special" rabbit that must not be chased or harmed in any way.

Gradually allow more and more freedom between the two pets until they seem to be getting along well. (Muzzling your dog is highly recommended until you are completely confident that it will not harm the rabbit.) It may take a couple of months, but if you are consistent, you should see results.

Keep in mind that some dogs, no matter how hard their owners try, can never be taught not to chase or attack a rabbit. Their predatory instincts are simply too strong. In these cases, you will either have to keep the dog permanently separated from the rabbit, return the rabbit to his breeder or take him to a foster home.

RABBIT ESSENTIALS

- hutch or cage
- nestbox
- food dish
- water bottle
- hay rack
- food (pellets, hay, fresh greens)
- litter box and litter
- straw or wood shavings for bedding
- chewing blocks
- toys
- travel carrier
- slicker or pin brush
- flea comb
- nail trimmer

Cats

Cats are usually better companions for rabbits than dogs primarily because the two species are similar in size. While cats are predators and are often inclined to

chase rabbits, they are less capable of doing damage than dogs, who can kill a rabbit with one snap of the jaw.

When preparing to introduce your cat and your rabbit, start out by buying a harness for your cat. Having your cat wear the harness during the no-cage introduction will give you control over her should she become combative. You should also have a water-filled squirt gun handy in case your cat gets out of hand.

Your cats, while sure to be very curious, will probably welcome the company of your new rabbit.

Using a nail trimmer, clip the claws on your cat's front paws. Should your cat become aggressive toward the rabbit, she will do little harm if her claws are dull.

Start out by showing the rabbit to your cat while the rabbit is still in his cage. The two animals will be very wary of each other at first, and the rabbit may hide in his nestbox.

If your cat approaches tentatively and does not behave aggressively toward the rabbit, reward her. If the cat hisses and runs away, ignore her. She will undoubtedly come back to investigate and will eventually get used to the intruder. If the cat reaches her arm into the cage and tries to get at the rabbit, squirt her with the water pistol from a distance. This will let her know that aggressive behavior toward the rabbit is not acceptable.

Once the two animals begin to ignore each other, you'll know that you are ready for the next step. Allow your rabbit out of his cage, with your cat on the harness. When the rabbit hops, the cat may move toward him as if to chase him. Don't allow this. Instead, keep the cat still and let her watch the rabbit move around the room until she gets used to the idea that she's not allowed to chase. You will need to repeat these getting-acquainted sessions on a regular basis until both animals are comfortable with each other. It may take some time, but in most cases, your efforts will pay off.

Once the rabbit has had a chance to get used to the cat, he will probably learn to ignore her, but there is a chance he will behave aggressively when the cat comes too close.

If your rabbit does behave aggressively toward your cat, let your cat get away from the rabbit. A cat who feels attacked and cornered will strike out and possibly hurt the rabbit. If your rabbit repeatedly seeks out your cat and attacks her for no apparent reason, you will have to teach your rabbit not to behave this way. Use the squirt-gun method mentioned above to help the rabbit understand that inappropriate aggression toward other animals in the home is unacceptable.

Other Rabbits

Fostering cohabitation between two rabbits is even more complicated than encouraging it among a dog and cat. In the wild, rabbits live with their own kind in complex societies. Whenever a rabbit is introduced to a member of its own species, the two lagomorphs have to figure out just where in the pecking order each one of them fits.

The first step toward a successful friendship among rabbits is spaying and neutering. Raging hormones can cause an intact rabbit to fight with another rabbit with whom it might normally get along. Spaying and neutering eliminates hormones from the equation, making rabbits calmer and more docile with one another.

When deciding whether or not two rabbits will become friends, keep in mind that gender can be an important factor. Spayed females and neutered males tend to get along better than other gender combinations. In most situations, however, rabbits who are strangers will behave assertively toward each other, regardless of

gender. This is why it is necessary to allow them to gradually get used to one another.

Begin by finding a place of neutral territory, where neither rabbit has had a chance to stake a claim, such as a room in the house where neither has ever been. Placing the rabbits on unclaimed turf will temper their instinctive urge to defend territory against one another.

If you plan to have more than one rabbit, know that their social instincts will lead them to establish a pecking order.

Keep the rabbits in their individual cages at first, and put the cages next to each other. Leave them together like this as often as possible. Once they seem used to each other, you can place them together in the neutral territory while both are on harnesses. Keep them from getting too close to each other, but allow them to spend as much time together this way as you can.

Once their tensions have subsided and they seem less hostile toward each other, let them get a little closer together while still on their leashes. This way, if they do attack each other, you will have control and can separate them.

Eventually, you can allow them to run together in the neutral space. There might be some fighting, but you can break it up by squirting your water gun. The rabbits will eventually work it out between themselves and will learn to tolerate each other, or hopefully, become fast friends.

Indoor Rabbits

It's impossible to truly appreciate life with a rabbit unless you keep it inside your home. Just like a dog or a cat, rabbits are companion animals with personalities all their own. If you don't actually live with a rabbit, day in and day out, you'll never get to know her as well as you could. Likewise, the rabbit won't get to know you as well either.

There are also many other, practical reasons for keeping a rabbit indoors. Rabbits who live inside tend to live longer than outdoor rabbits. Illness is another cause of death in outdoor rabbits, since they are more difficult to monitor. Signs of sickness can be subtle at first, and it can be a day or so before illness is even recognized.

Housing

Even though your indoor rabbit will have a roof over her head in a literal sense, she'll still need her own private retreat. A cage can offer security for your rabbit and can also offer her privacy and a safe haven. Cages are useful during litter box training and while your rabbit is learning to behave herself around the house.

ADVANTAGES OF INDOOR HOUSING

- You can train your rabbit to use a litter box and avoid cleaning a large outdoor hutch.
- You get to know your pet's personality better when you spend more time with her.
- Your rabbit will be a constant companion, not just an outdoor pet.
- You don't have to worry about the effects of inclement weather on your rabbit's health and well-being.
- It's easier to monitor your rabbit's health when she's indoors with you; indoor rabbits live longer.

Indoor rabbit cages are readily available in a wide variety of styles in pet supply stores and through catalogs. When searching for just the right cage for your indoor rabbit, look for one made from sturdy wire with a removable bottom tray. Your rabbit will not gnaw on the wire, and the removable tray will make cleaning easier. Wire will also allow your pet to receive the ventilation and light that she needs while confined.

Look for a cage that is well put together and easy to disassemble for cleaning. The cage should have a door on top so you can reach inside. It should also have a door on the side so the rabbit can go in and out of the cage whenever she wishes.

The mesh on the cage wire (top and sides) should be no more than one by two inches in size, since anything larger is dangerous to your rabbit. A leg or head could get caught in mesh that is too big.

Cage Flooring

If your indoor rabbit will be litter box trained, there is no need for the traditional wire mesh floor usually seen in outdoor hutches. In this case, the floor of the indoor rabbit cage can be solid, either rustproof metal or hard plastic. A solid floor is useful if you choose not to provide your pet with a nestbox, since it can also accommodate loose bedding such as straw, shavings or a blanket.

It is acceptable for indoor rabbit cages to have wire flooring, if this is the style you prefer. Make sure the wire is galvanized with the smooth side down. The mesh should be about one by one-half inches in size. Wire is uncomfortable for a rabbit's feet, and prolonged time on wire floors can result in sore hocks. For this reason, a piece of wood (any type except redwood, which is toxic to rabbits) should be placed in the cage to give the rabbit a place to sit off the wire.

Cage Size

If your indoor rabbit will spend a lot of time loose in the house and not in her cage, she will not need as big an enclosure as would her outdoor counterpart. Even if this is the case, the indoor cage should still be big enough for the rabbit to stretch out and hop around in while also accommodating a small litter box, an area for sleeping far from the litter box, food and water accessories and a toy or two. The height of the cage should also allow the rabbit to stand up on her hind legs without her ears touching the top. If you plan to include a nestbox, be sure the cage is tall enough to hold the box.

Your indoor rabbit's cage should house all of her necessities: litter box, food, water and toys.

If your rabbit is very young, you may want to consider buying a smaller cage, since indoor rabbit cages are relatively inexpensive. You can then purchase a bigger one later on when your rabbit is fully grown (at about six months of age, depending on the breed).

Nestboxes

Rabbits are burrowing animals by nature. In the wild, they live under the ground in dens that they dig for themselves. These burrows provide them with a sense of well-being and security. For this reason, rabbits who live above ground as pets enjoy having nestboxes, a substitute for burrows, inside their cages.

Never question whether a curious rabbit will get into things she shouldn't—she will!

A nestbox is a small boxlike enclosure with an entry hole cut into it that contains the animal's bedding, and provides a safe place to sleep and hide. A cardboard box can work as a nestbox. However, most rabbits will chew a cardboard nestbox to pieces, so wood is preferable. Commercially made nestboxes are available through pet supply outlets and mail order catalogs that specialize in rabbit supplies, or you can build your own nestbox.

Your rabbit's nestbox should be big enough for the animal to turn around in while several inches of bedding (straw or wood shavings) are in place. Make sure the entrance to the nestbox is big enough for your rabbit to gain entry, and that one side of the box is removable so you can clean it.

Cage Location

When determining where in the house to place your rabbit's cage, remember that heat is an extremely dangerous element for rabbits. Do not put your rabbit's cage in a spot where the sun will shine directly on it, and avoid keeping it near a radiator, stove, fireplace or other heating element.

While heat is hazardous to a rabbit's health, cold drafts can also be deadly. Keep your rabbit's cage away from doors and windows, where winter drafts can leak in through joints. Try to keep your rabbit's cage off the floor during cold weather, too, since cold air tends to lie near the ground, creating drafts.

Avoid placing your rabbit's cage in dark and damp areas. Basements and garages are not usually suitable areas for rabbits, since these places in the home typically have minimal light, poor ventilation and excess moisture. Garages are also dangerous because rabbits are sensitive to automobile exhaust.

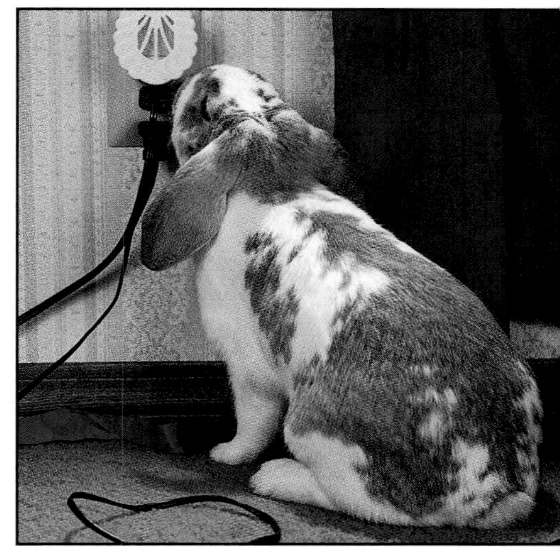

Your rabbit-proofing should include either covering electrical cords with plastic or putting them out of the rabbit's reach.

Try to find a place in your home where your rabbit will be able to watch household activity without being unduly disturbed. You want your rabbit to feel like part of the family, so her cage needs to be in a room where people come and go. However, don't put her in such a busy spot that she will never be able to rest or relax. Be especially careful not to place her cage near a television set, stereo or radio. A rabbit's hearing is very sensitive, and constant noise can be very disturbing to your pet.

Rabbit-Proofing

Because rabbits are gnawing mammals and have an innate need to chew, it is vitally important that you rabbit-proof your home before you let your rabbit run loose. Rabbits will chew on electrical cords, carpeting and anything made out of wood. Along with providing your rabbit with toys that she can chew on, you'll also need to devise ways to keep your rabbit from gnawing on household items, for the sake of your home and your rabbit's health.

Electrical Cords

Electrical cords pose the greatest threat to the safety of your rabbit, and should be of primary concern.

Rabbits can and will chew through electrical cords, risking the chance of electrocuting themselves and causing a fire hazard in your home. You can protect your home and your rabbit by moving dangling cords up out of reach. Cords that cannot be moved should be covered with plastic aquarium-type tubing: Slit the tubing lengthwise and put the cord inside of it. Or, you can try wrapping the cord with spiral cable wrap available in electronic stores.

Wooden Surfaces

Wooden corners and other chewable areas that will be attractive to your rabbit can be covered with thick plastic or treated with an odoriferous substance. Perfume and cologne are very repugnant to rabbits, who have a sharp sense of smell. Store-bought repellents made to keep away other pets can also be used. Not all rabbits will be rebuffed by this however, and you may have to resort to covering problem areas with an unchewable surface.

Digging

In addition to being compulsive chewers, rabbits are also vehement diggers. In the wild, rabbits must excavate to create and maintain their burrows. This instinct is alive and well in domestic rabbits and must be addressed with regard to the indoor pet.

One way your rabbit may choose to express her digging instinct will be to assail your carpeting. She'll find a spot where the carpet separates from the wall and proceed to dig it up. She may even chew on the fibers, which could prove disastrous to her digestive system.

Encourage your rabbit to excavate elsewhere by providing her with a box of soil that she can dig in to her heart's content. Place the box in the bathtub or other area of the house where the dirt won't fly everywhere. Then, when your rabbit begins to tunnel through the carpet, gently pick her up and place her in the box of dirt. You can also try firmly tacking the carpeting down and treating it with an odorous repellent to discourage her from returning to that area.

Nooks, Crannies and Other Hazards

Another important part of rabbit-proofing your home is taking a survey of all the places where your rabbit could get caught or hide. Since rabbits are very inquisitive animals, you can be sure that your pet will explore every nook and cranny of your house. Look around for rabbit-size spaces that your pet could escape through or get trapped in. Block these areas up securely. While you're busy surveying the house, make sure that toxic household chemicals and trash bags are well hidden from your pet.

Make sure all cleaning supplies are stored in a cabinet to which your rabbit doesn't have access.

Litter Box Training

One of the reasons that rabbits make excellent indoor pets is their receptivity to litter box training. The rabbit's denning instinct, which it inherited from its wild ancestors, is responsible for this inherent behavior. Rabbits, just like cats and dogs, prefer not to foul the area where they eat and sleep and will instead venture out of their "dens" to relieve themselves.

Some rabbits are easy to train to use the litter box, while others require more time and patience. The most important things to remember when litter box training a rabbit are consistency and praise. Never scold your rabbit for not using the litter box, since this will only frighten and confuse her. Another important point is to work gradually, starting your rabbit out in a small space and then moving up to giving her run of the whole house.

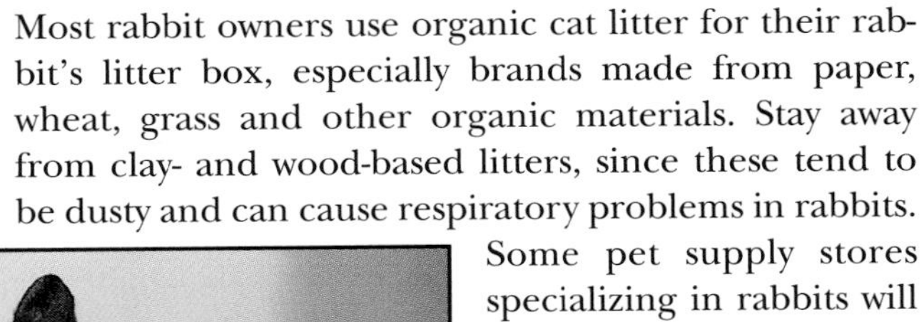

Most rabbit owners use organic cat litter for their rabbit's litter box, especially brands made from paper, wheat, grass and other organic materials. Stay away from clay- and wood-based litters, since these tend to be dusty and can cause respiratory problems in rabbits. Some pet supply stores specializing in rabbits will carry litter made just for them. This variety is the best type to buy. You can also use straw on top of a layer of newspaper as litter, although it will be less absorbent than most commercially made brands.

It's a good idea to place a few extra litter boxes around the house when you first begin training your rabbit to use one.

Start the litter box training process in a very small area, preferably the rabbit's cage. Place a small litter box (the same type used for cats) in a corner of your rabbit's cage, attached to the side with a clip or twistable wire for removal when cleaning. Try to place the box in the area of the cage that your rabbit tends to use most frequently for elimination. Put some fecal pellets in the box to help give her the right idea and then add a handful of hay to a corner of the box to encourage her to use it.

Don't be alarmed if the rabbit sits in the box and munches on the hay you've placed in it, since rabbits will often eat and defecate simultaneously. Munching on the hay will stimulate your rabbit's digestive system and may cause her to use the box just as you intended. If, however, your rabbit prefers to sleep in her litter box rather than use it as a toilet, you may want to provide her with a more attractive bed than the one she has. Try using a different bedding material.

Moving Beyond the Cage

Once your rabbit seems to be using the litter box in her cage and has been allowed to do so for some time, you can then try giving her a little more space. Create a special part of the house just for her. (Kitchens, bathrooms or hallways work best.) Use a baby gate to section off a small area so you can still keep an eye on your rabbit.

Place the litter box in the small area, along with the rabbit's food, water and bedding. Watch your rabbit to make sure that she uses the litter box on a regular basis. If she is using the litter box successfully, then you can increase the amount of space in the house that is accessible to her.

The more often you clean your rabbit's litter box, the easier the task will be.

If your rabbit starts making mistakes at any point in the process, then it may have been too soon to place her in a bigger area. Return her to her cage and start over. Or, you may want to try buying a few more litter boxes and placing them in various parts of the rabbit's space. With so many litter box options to choose from, she is bound to get the right idea. You can then try gradually removing all of the boxes except one. In the meantime, clean up after your pet by picking up fecal pellets with a tissue, and washing urine marks on carpeting with a mixture of vinegar and water. Urine on wood floors can be cleaned simply with soap and water.

Litter Box Cleaning

When it's time to clean your rabbit's litter box (once or twice a week), use a water and vinegar solution, and dry it thoroughly before filling it with litter and returning it to its usual spot.

chapter 6

Outdoor Rabbits

If keeping your rabbit indoors is out of the question, it is possible to successfully house your rabbit outside if you take strict precautions. Before you prepare to bring your outdoor rabbit home with you, be sure to check your local zoning ordinances to make sure it is legal to keep a rabbit outdoors in your area.

Housing

When determining what kind of housing you will provide for your rabbit, and where it will be located, there are many details you must keep in mind in order to keep your rabbit healthy and safe.

Your first concern is the weather. You must protect your rabbit from the elements, as well as from extreme changes in temperature. You will also need to guard against predators, and allow your rabbit enough room to move around comfortably.

The Hutch

There are a number of commercially made hutches available on the market that are specifically designed for rabbits. It's important to choose a hutch that will meet your rabbit's needs for shelter, comfort and safety.

SIZE

First, consider size. The more room you can provide for your rabbit, the better. Buy your rabbit the largest hutch that your allotted space will accommodate.

When determining a suitable living space for a rabbit, keep your pet's size in mind. If you will be bringing home a baby or immature rabbit, find out or imagine how big he will grow to be.

Rabbits can live comfortably outdoors when housed in a proper hutch.

A good rule of thumb when determining the minimum living room your rabbit will need is to calculate one square foot of space for each pound of rabbit. For example, a nine-pound Rex needs at least nine square feet of cage space (three feet by three feet). However, it is preferable to give your rabbit even more room than this. A rabbit that does not have enough room in his hutch may become depressed. Too small a space will also be fouled more quickly with feces and urine, leaving the rabbit to spend more time than he should in unsanitary conditions. On the other hand, don't get a single-door hutch that is so deep that you can't reach

into it to clean it. Large hutches should have more than one access door.

You'll also want to make sure that your hutch is big enough to accommodate a separate sleeping space, either in the form of a nestbox or a built-in compartment. Providing your rabbit with a secluded and separate place to sleep will help him feel safer and happier in his hutch. A built-in sleeping compartment should be about one-and-a-half feet long and half a foot in height and width for small rabbits; two-and-a-half feet long and around nine inches in height and width for medium rabbits and two feet long and about a foot in height and width for large rabbits.

Built-in sleeping compartments or nestboxes will help your rabbit stay cozy in his outdoor accommodations.

Materials

Most rabbit hutches are made from either wood and wire or just wire. Each type has its advantages and disadvantages.

Wooden rabbit hutches usually consist of a wooden roof and several wood-panel sides, with wire mesh on the door, front and/or some sides of the cage. Wooden hutches stay cooler in the summer and warmer in the winter, provided that they are made with a good quality wood and not pressboard. They can also be very attractive.

However, since wood exposed to the elements is prone to rotting, the hutch will likely fall apart after some time. Another disadvantage to wood is that rabbits love to chew on it and can gnaw sections of a wooden hutch to pieces if the wood is not protected by wire mesh.

Metal hutches, on the other hand, have the disadvantage of retaining heat in the summer and cold in the winter, both of which can be harmful to the rabbit. Metal hutches are very durable, however, and can last a very long time if they are well-made. They are also easier to clean than wood hutches and are frequently less expensive.

Hutch Specifications

Whether you choose a wooden hutch or a wire hutch, it's important to select a home for your rabbit that utilizes the proper type of wire. Chicken wire is not acceptable, since it is flimsy and easily removed by both the rabbit and by predators. Side panels and doors on both wooden and metal hutches should be made from sturdy, galvanized wire, around fourteen gauge in weight. The size of the holes in the wire mesh should be no larger than one by two inches.

The roof of an outdoor hutch should be covered with a waterproof substance, such as heavy-duty plastic or roofing material. This is vital if the hutch and its occupant are to stay warm and dry in inclement weather.

Floor materials are very important in a hutch. Improper flooring can cause your rabbit to develop a number of health problems. Most hutches have some wire flooring, designed to allow feces and urine to drop down away from the rabbit. However, wire mesh that is too large can be dangerous, since the rabbit's foot may fall through. The wire mesh should also be smooth, since a rough edge can result in sore hocks.

ADVANTAGES OF OUTDOOR HOUSING

- Litter box training isn't necessary.
- You don't have to deal with urine spraying inside the house.
- Your rabbit can watch outdoor activity and be stimulated even when no one in the family is home.
- You don't run the risk of your rabbit chewing on your walls and furniture or digging in your floors or carpeting.
- Your rabbit doesn't have to get along with your other pets.

With these things taken into consideration, it is best to get a hutch with a floor made of one-half-inch-by-one-inch, fourteen-gauge, welded wire. Last but not least, make sure that at least one-third of the floor space contains a flat, porous surface (preferably wood) where your rabbit can sit to get off the wire.

Design

When considering which hutch to purchase for an outdoor rabbit, the factors of rabbit health, safety and comfort mentioned above obviously come into play. Beyond this, however, the choice of design in a hutch is a matter of individual preference based on convenience, quality and aesthetic appeal.

Quality

The first feature to look for in hutch design is quality. Does the hutch appear to be well built? Is it made from quality materials? Look to see that the welding was done before the metal was galvanized. Check the hinges and various connections throughout the hutch to determine whether they are well put together. Examine the construction carefully to make sure that the hutch is secure and escape-proof. Feel around the hutch for sharp points. Unfinished edges indicate sloppy handiwork and a potential danger to your rabbit.

Height

Another element to consider is height. Some hutches are made low to the ground, while others have legs that put them anywhere from several inches to several feet off the ground. It's always best, in the interest of better ventilation and sanitation, if the hutch is at least six inches off the ground. Hutches that rest directly on the soil invite rodents to nest underneath the floor. So, if you purchase a hutch with no legs, keep in mind that you'll have to create some means of raising it up to allow air to pass underneath.

If you do buy a hutch with legs, the most desirable kind is one where the bottom of the cage is at waist height.

This kind of hutch is far easier to clean and allows easier access to the rabbit. In addition, unless you do decide to get a hutch that is particularly low to the ground, avoid models with a top-opening door and opt for the kind with a door in the front. This will also help you clean the hutch and access the rabbit with more convenience.

To ensure that the hutch fits the needs of their pet, many rabbit owners will actually design and build their own outdoor hutch. If you choose to do this, you may want to contact your local county extension office or the American Rabbit Breeders Association for plans and further information on how to construct a safe and sturdy hutch. (See Chapter 12 for more information on how to contact ARBA.)

Location

Temperature and Sunlight Heat is more dangerous to rabbits than cold, so when choosing a location for your hutch, make sure it is in a shady spot. Temperatures above eighty degrees are considered dangerous for rabbits, especially if accompanied by high humidity. On the other hand, you don't want to keep your rabbit in total darkness, either. Pick a location with moderate sun exposure, but one in which the rabbit has sufficient shade to keep him out of direct sunlight.

A well-placed hutch will have some exposure to sunlight, but will also have adequate shade.

While rabbits are better able to tolerate cold than heat, they should still be protected from drafts, as well as from dampness. Constant wind or drafts are likely to cause your rabbit to get sick; hot, humid weather can cause moldy, unsanitary conditions in the nesting box; and rain or snow can drench a rabbit and his entire bed. Choose a

protected location for your rabbit hutch where it is out of drafts and wind. Placing it alongside a building can often provide defense from the wind.

Aside from keeping the rabbit away from direct sunlight and from taking him indoors, one way to protect your rabbit from overheating in the summertime is to provide him with plastic jugs of frozen water that he can lay against to keep cool. Keep a few of these jugs on hand in your freezer so you can rotate them once the ice melts.

Your rabbit will be happiest when allowed to romp around in the grass every so often—with supervision, of course!

Ventilation Ventilation is also an important factor in hutch placement. Caged rabbits need plenty of fresh air since a stuffy environment can wreak havoc on a rabbit's respiratory system. The ammonia from the rabbit's urine and the dust from its bedding can cause respiratory distress and infection, causing the rabbit to become sick and even die. Make sure you select a spot that, while still protected from the elements, is well ventilated.

Peace and Quiet Also in the interest of the rabbit's well-being, don't place your hutch in a place where there is excessive noise. Rabbits like to nap during the day and will become nervous and stressed if there are frequent loud noises or disturbances.

Convenience and Security When choosing a spot for your rabbit's home, keep in mind that you will need to have convenient access to it so you can clean it regularly, give food to your rabbit and take him out daily for exercise and companionship.

It's also important to keep in mind that rabbits are prey animals and will attract any number of predators. Dogs and cats are only two of the creatures that will be drawn to your yard once a rabbit is in place.

Depending on where you live, raccoons, coyotes and even weasels may try to invade your rabbit's hutch.

Rabbit cages can be kept on apartment terraces as long as the space is protected just as it would be in a backyard. Provide shade for the hutch and safeguards from climbing predators, as well as protection from drafts and temperature extremes.

Outdoor Rabbit Care

Rabbits that are housed outdoors need special attention. The most important aspect of outdoor rabbit care is observation. Since your rabbit is outside, you must be devoted to making time to spend time with him.

As is true with humans, the early treatment of an illness can often mean the difference between life or death to a rabbit. Learn to recognize how he behaves when he is feeling good so you will immediately be aware when there is a problem.

Rabbits' denning instincts lead them to dig voraciously; you'll be glad when your rabbit's material of choice is dirt, not your carpet.

Exercise

It's important that your rabbit receive daily exercise. If you cannot bring him inside the house to play, then you'll have to provide him with a completely enclosed run in the backyard to stretch his legs (the bigger the better, with six feet being the minimum length for a medium-size rabbit). If your yard is enclosed by walls or a sturdy fence with no holes that a rabbit can slip through, you may give him the run of the yard. However, a rabbit should never run loose without supervision since he may fall victim to a predator or poisonous plants in your yard. Since rabbits are excellent diggers, it's even possible that you rabbit may dig a tunnel right out of your yard if you're not watching him.

Social Interaction

Since rabbits are highly social creatures, an outdoor rabbit living alone in a hutch can suffer terribly from loneliness. For this reason, you will need to make a concerted effort to provide him with social interaction. Bring him in the house as often as you can so he can spend time with you. Sit out in the backyard with him as he plays in his run or in the yard. And if you don't have a lot of time to do this, get another rabbit to keep him company in his hutch.

Regular Cleaning

Outdoor hutches get dirty quickly, and for your rabbit's health and well-being, you'll need to clean your hutch frequently. While you can get away with not cleaning it every day, it wouldn't hurt to do so. Time spent cleaning the hutch is also a good opportunity to inspect the inside of the structure for damage.

A rabbit needs social interaction, either with you or another rabbit, to stay healthy and happy.

Before you clean the hutch, remove your rabbit and put him in a safe place. (A travel carrier is useful for this purpose.) Don't let him roam about unsupervised, since he may get into trouble while you are working.

Because rabbits normally live in dens, they tend to pick a specific area of their hutch to use for elimination. Using a spatula and hand shovel, scrape away the feces and urine that has built up in that area. Once a week, you should also scrub the area with a hard bristle brush and water mixed with a splash of bleach. Wait until the inside of the hutch is completely dry before placing the rabbit back in it.

chapter 7

Nutrition and Grooming

Rabbits are relatively easy pets to care for once you have taken the time to learn about their health requirements. While dogs, cats and humans all share a similar physiological makeup, rabbits actually have a great deal in common with horses in the way their bodies work. For this reason, you will have to make a concerted effort to learn about the dietary needs of your rabbit, which differ from the dietary needs of the ordinary pets and from your own.

Feeding

What you feed your rabbit can mean the difference between a healthy, long-lived pet and a sickly, unhappy animal. Rabbits are

herbivores; they eat only plant material. In nature, this characteristic causes the rabbit to be a grazer, or an animal who spends considerable amounts of time foraging for and eating plants. Because plant material is difficult to break down, the digestive tract of the rabbit is uniquely constructed.

It's important to give your rabbit a diet that simulates that which she would eat in the wild. Otherwise, your rabbit could end up with chronic diarrhea; heart, liver and kidney disease; and obesity, which vets find to the be biggest health problem among domestic rabbits.

FEEDING DO'S AND DON'TS

- Feed pellets to your rabbit, but don't feed them exclusive of other important foods, such as hay and greens.
- Avoid overfeeding, which can cause obesity.
- Store pellet feed in the refrigerator to maintain freshness.
- Never feed your rabbit hay that shows signs of mold.
- Feed your rabbit two times a day and leave a handful of hay in the hay rack at all times.
- Wash your rabbit's food bowls frequently to avoid bacteria buildup.
- Feed your rabbit timothy hay, if available; if not, alfalfa hay is acceptable.
- Offer your rabbit fresh greens every day.
- Keep your rabbit's water bottle full at all times.
- Don't make abrupt changes in your rabbit's diet.
- Feed your rabbit treats, preferably fresh fruits, in moderation.
- Don't prevent your rabbit from eating the cecotropes produced by her large intestine; these are an important source of nutrients.
- Keep the feeding schedule regular.

PELLETS

Many people still believe that rabbits only need to eat pellets. This is a myth and is one of the reasons why there are so many overweight pet rabbits. While pellets are a valuable staple in a rabbit's diet, this type of food is not all a rabbit should be eating. Pelletized feed should make up only a small portion of what your rabbit eats.

When purchasing a pelletized rabbit feed, look for a product that contains at least eighteen percent fiber. Read the packaging to be sure that the pellets are labeled "nutritionally complete."

Do not buy a large supply of pellets, since they can go bad over time. Purchase as much as your rabbit will consume in about a month. Storing them in the refrigerator will help keep them fresh.

How Much at What Age and Size

If your rabbit is young (under eight months of age), you may leave a bowl of pellets in the cage at all times for her to eat at will. However, if you have an adult, you should only provide two feedings of pellets per day, since they are high in calories.

The size of your rabbit will determine how much pelletized feed you give her. If your pet is a dwarf or small rabbit weighing between two and four pounds, you should provide her with one ounce of pellets per day. If your small rabbit weighs between five and seven pounds, two ounces is sufficient.

Medium-size rabbits weighing between eight and ten pounds can get four ounces per day. Large- and giant-breed rabbits who weigh in at eleven to fifteen pounds can get six ounces per day. (Remember to split the number of ounces per day in half for each feeding.)

If your rabbit does not eat the pellets you place in her dish, throw the old ones away before you refill the bowl. It's important for your rabbit to only be offered fresh pellets. Likewise, remember to wash out your rabbit's food dish every so often to prevent the build-up of bacteria that often develops in unwashed food containers.

The amount of pelletized feed you give your rabbit will depend on its size.

Hay

When you purchased your rabbit's cage or hutch, you also bought a hay rack. The reason for this was that rabbits need free access to fibrous foods, and hay, which is pure roughage, fits the bill.

Hay can be obtained from a number of sources, including pet supply stores, feed stores and local horse stables. When you purchase hay, check it for freshness.

Good, clean hay should have a sweet smell and a minimum of dust. Examine it for mold, which can be very harmful to rabbits if ingested.

There are different types of hay available on the market. Your pet supply store will stock packaged alfalfa and timothy hay, while feed stores and stables will have baled hay. **Timothy hay** is generally the best of these choices. If your rabbit is eating pellets, **alfalfa hay** is already included in her diet, and the addition of more may cause her to become overweight. (Hay cubes are not recommended for rabbits.)

Offer your rabbit fresh greens in addition to water, pellets and hay, to provide her with a nutritious diet.

Give your rabbit a handful of fresh hay every day to keep her digestive system in working order. Place the hay in the hay rack to help keep it from scattering all around the cage. Remove old hay from the cage and the rack before you replace it with new hay.

Greens

Fresh greens are another important dietary element that should be provided daily.

Some of the best greens for rabbits include dark leaf romaine lettuce, dandelions, carrot tops, broccoli, basil, spinach, celery and artichokes. Many other green leafy vegetables that humans eat are good for rabbits too, provided the leaves are dark green in color.

Make sure the greens you offer your rabbit are fresh, and be sure to wash them thoroughly to remove residual pesticides.

A Garden for Your Rabbit

You may want to consider growing a garden for your rabbit where she can hop around outside foraging for greens as nature intended. Good garden plants that are healthy for rabbits include coltsfoot, dandelion, dead-nettles, ground elder, mugwort, plantain, ragwort, shepherd's purse and yarrow. Rabbits also like to nibble on Bermuda grass and clover.

To create a rabbit garden, set aside a patch of your backyard and plant the seeds of some of the abovenamed plants. Use organic soil and no pesticides. When the plants are mature, create a protective enclosure for your rabbit. Then let your rabbit run loose among the plants to graze to her heart's content.

Growing a garden especially for your rabbit is a good way to provide her with both needed nutrients and needed activity.

If your rabbit is a strictly indoor rabbit, you can grow some of these same plants in a large tray on your balcony or fire escape. Bring the tray inside every so often and let your rabbit munch on the plants. She will enjoy the opportunity to harvest her own greens, and you will have fun observing her.

Let your rabbit visit the garden or tray once or twice a week. On the other days, be sure to provide her with different greens than the ones you are growing in your garden so she will have needed diversity.

If your rabbit is not used to eating fresh foods, you should introduce them gradually to her diet so as not to cause a bout of diarrhea. Start out by offering her one new item of food once per week. Eventually, your rabbit should be receiving three different types of fresh greens daily, at one cup per five pounds of rabbit.

It is possible that your rabbit will have a sensitivity to a particular vegetable; you'll know if she gets diarrhea shortly after she eats it. Should this happen, remove the offending food from her diet.

TREATS

Natural Treats The healthiest treats to feed your rabbit are fresh fruits. Some types of treats that rabbits enjoy include apples, pears, strawberries, peaches and tomatoes. While these items are particularly popular among rabbits, you can offer your pet just about any fruit. Just be sure to offer them in moderation.

Rabbits love most any fruit; offer them as a nutritious snack.

Commercially Prepared Treats Commercially prepared treats can also be acceptable for rabbits, as long as the treats are not overfed. Avoid giving your rabbit commercial treats that contain sugar. Do *not* give your pet traditional human treats that are high in sugar or salt, including chocolate.

Twigs and Branches You may also want to occasionally provide some dried and aged twigs from an unsprayed fruit tree to your rabbit as a treat. Rabbits love to gnaw on branches and sometimes rip off the bark and eat it. (Finding twigs that are dried and aged is important since some tree branches are poisonous when fresh.)

Cecotropes Several decades ago, researchers discovered that rabbits have an unusual way of supplementing their diet. Small, soft pellets known as cecotropes are produced by the rabbit's cecum (a part of its large intestine). These cecotropes, which contain special nutrients, pass from the anus and are then instinctively eaten by the rabbit. While this may seem very strange to us, nature developed this process as a way of aiding the rabbit's ability to absorb nutrients from the hard-to-digest cellulose material contained in plants.

In order for your rabbit to get the most nutrition from her diet, she must be able to consume an adequate amount of the cecotropes produced by her body. Since these pellets are usually ingested just as they leave the anus, you may see your rabbit eating them as they are produced. Do not try to discourage her from acting on this instinct, which usually takes place during the evening hours.

Dried twigs are a great treat for a rabbit to gnaw on.

If for some reason your rabbit is not able to eat the cecotropes produced by her body, she could become seriously ill. Make sure your rabbit is provided with a solid place in her cage to sit, since rabbits who live in cages with floors that are constructed strictly of wire often have difficulty consuming their cecotropes.

Other Items While many pet supply stores stock salt licks for use in rabbit cages, most rabbits do not need salt blocks if they are on a diet that includes pellets. Pellets that are nutritionally complete contain salt as a part of their ingredients. Providing a salt block cannot hurt your rabbit, however, and you can offer her one to see if she likes it.

Rabbits who are healthy and eating a balanced diet do not need vitamins added to their feed. Should your rabbit ever become ill or greatly stressed, your veterinarian may recommend a diet supplement on a temporary basis, but you need not otherwise provide supplementation.

WATER

Water is very important to maintain the health of a rabbit, and should be provided at all times. Many rabbits will drink nearly a quart of water a day. Change your rabbit's water daily and wash the water bottle out on a regular basis.

Grooming

One of the first things you will notice when you start living with your rabbit is that she loves to groom herself. Rabbits are much like cats in that respect and are always preening and primping.

However, there are some grooming tasks you will need to take on for your rabbit. Since rabbits do shed, an overabundance of loose hairs can wind up in the animal's digestive tract, swallowed during the process of self-grooming. Grooming also provides you with a chance to look your rabbit over for any signs of parasites or ill health.

Rabbits love to groom themselves.

It is best to set aside an hour once a week for grooming. (Longhaired breeds must be groomed every day.) Using the tools you purchased, find a comfortable spot where you can sit with your rabbit on your lap.

Begin by brushing or combing your rabbit. If you notice that a lot of loose hairs are coming out, and it is spring or fall, your rabbit may be molting. Molting is when a rabbit begins to lose much of her hair in preparation for the season to come. In the summertime, the hair falls out so the rabbit will have less coat. In the winter, the shedded hairs are replaced by more fur that will help keep the animal warm. During the molting seasons, it is best to brush your pet at least every other day.

If your rabbit has long hair, you will need to use your brush to work out any mats you may find in her coat. Regular and careful grooming will prevent mats from forming. Another option for longhaired rabbits is to have them shorn by a professional groomer experienced in handling rabbits.

Grooming Checklist

When you are brushing and combing your pet, keep an eye out for fleas. Rabbits are just as susceptible to fleas as dogs are, especially if they live or play outside. If you find fleas on your pet, contact your veterinarian for information on how to rid your rabbit of this pest. Your vet can provide you with rabbit-safe chemicals designed to kill fleas and give you details on how to eliminate fleas from your rabbit's environment.

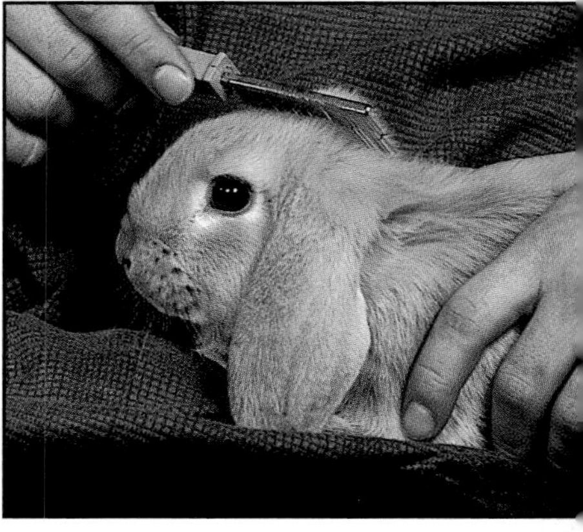

Rabbit coats need little else than regular combing or brushing to keep them in good shape.

As you brush or comb your rabbit, keep an eye out for any lumps or sores on the animal's body that could be an indication of disease or infection. Crusts and scabs suggest the presence of mites.

Check your rabbit's eyes and ears for any discharge while you are handling her. Examine the bottoms of her feet for sores and check under her chin to make sure that her scent gland is not swollen or infected.

Your rabbit's ears should also be attended to during the regular grooming session. Examine them for signs of waxy build-up or debris. Clean your pet's ears of wax with a solution that can be purchased from your veterinarian. Dark wax or the appearance of dirt in the ears can be a sign of ear mites.

If you own one of the lop-eared breeds, you will have to pay special attention to the ears during grooming time. Because an ear that hangs down instead of standing straight up is not natural, lop-eared rabbits are more prone to ear infections. Examine your lop's ears closely for excess wax build-up, debris or foul smell.

Trimming Nails

Trimming your rabbit's toenails is also a necessary part of your grooming sessions, although it will not need to be done every week. Check the length and condition of your rabbit's nails every time you groom her. Once they appear to be getting long, it is time to trim them.

Trim your rabbit's nails when you notice them getting long.

Prepare to trim your rabbit's nails by wrapping her in a towel and placing her gently in your lap, with her legs facing upward. Use your clipper to take off a portion of the nail. Be careful not to cut the quick in the toenail, since doing so can cause pain to the rabbit and a bloody toenail. A silhouette of the quick can be seen by holding the nail up to a light.

If you are nervous about trimming your rabbit's nails for the first time, or if your rabbit struggles when you try to hold her in your lap, you may want to ask your veterinarian to show you how to perform this necessary function the first time.

Avoid Bathing

Although you might be tempted, try to avoid giving your rabbit a bath. As a rule, rabbits don't enjoy being bathed and rarely need to have this done to them. If your rabbit needs her bottom cleaned, try to cleanse it with soap and water without submerging the entire rabbit in water.

chapter 8

Your Rabbit's Health

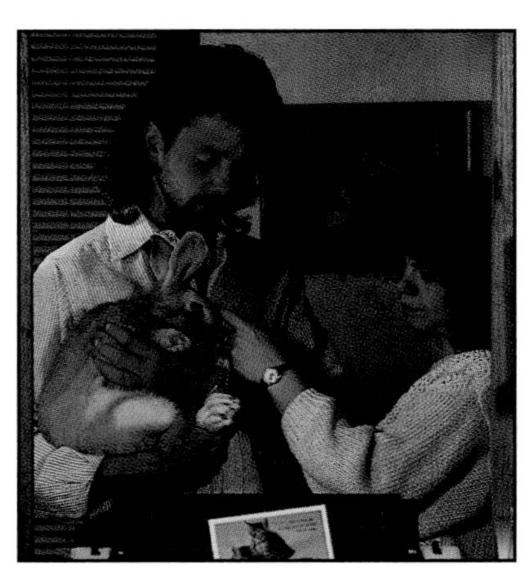

Rabbits who are well fed and properly cared for rarely get sick. However, if a rabbit's basic needs for a proper diet, a clean environment and regular exercise are not met, the animal will become susceptible to a number of dangerous illnesses.

In other words, taking good care of your rabbit will pay off in the long run. And, since many rabbit ailments are difficult to cure, prevention is the best policy.

Disease Prevention

If you follow the feeding and housing guidelines outlined in this book, your rabbit should live a long and healthy life. There are, however, extra precautions that you can use to ward off illnesses and ways to deal with problems effectively, should they come up.

Diet

Probably the single most important step to take in keeping your rabbit healthy is feeding him the proper diet. In order for the digestive system to work properly, your rabbit needs to eat certain foods. (See Chapter 7 for more information on this subject.) A correctly functioning digestive system will help your rabbit ward off a number of ailments that often trouble less well-kept animals.

When changing your rabbit's diet or adding a new food, remember to always do so gradually. A sudden alteration in your pet's diet can wreak havoc with his digestive system and cause him to become seriously ill.

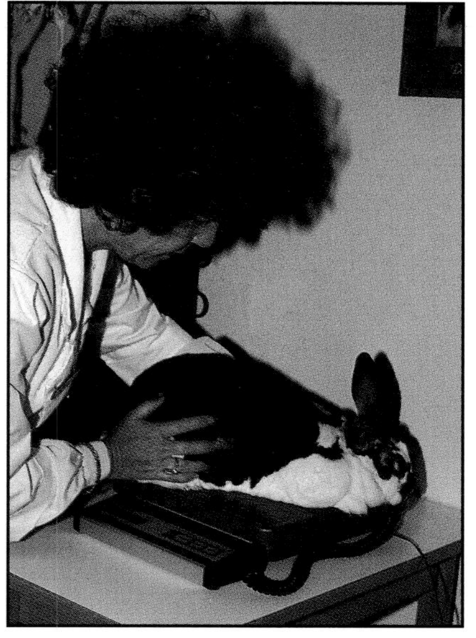

Veterinarians report that obesity is the number one health problem in rabbits.

It is also extremely important to see that your rabbit's diet contains an adequate amount of clean, fresh water. Dehydration can be a life-threatening condition in rabbits.

Cleanliness

While cleaning your rabbit's cage or hutch may be the last thing you want to do when you finally get a free moment in an otherwise busy day, it is a vital chore. An unsanitary cage is a breeding ground for disease. A number of different illnesses can be directly traced to dirty floors and nestboxes, and unclean food bowls and water bottles. Remove fouled bedding and fecal matter daily, and wash your cage or hutch once a week to keep the growth of bacteria at a minimum. Scrub out your rabbit's food dish and water bottle every day.

Stress

Rabbits are susceptible to stress just as humans are. Unlike most humans, however, your rabbit cannot do

much to change his life and alleviate his stress. He relies on you to do this for him.

Stress has serious consequences on the body's immune system. You may have noticed that when you are under a lot of stress, you tend to catch colds more easily. The same is true for rabbits, although the ailments they catch can be much more dangerous than the common cold.

It is for this reason that a rabbit's stress should be kept to a minimum. This means that the animal should not be exposed to loud noises, constant handling (especially by children), severe temperature changes and situations that will cause it to be frightened.

Finding a Veterinarian

Since your rabbit's body differs considerably from that of a cat or dog, some of the treatments and medications appropriate for these other pets could be harmful to your rabbit. Given this, it's important to use only a vet who has experience in treating rabbits.

Make sure that the vet you choose is practiced in treating rabbits.

No matter what kind of pet you own, it's best not to wait until you have an emergency on your hands to go looking for a veterinarian. Since vets who specialize in treating rabbits are harder to find than traditional small animal doctors, it is wise to select your rabbit's veterinarian before he actually needs one.

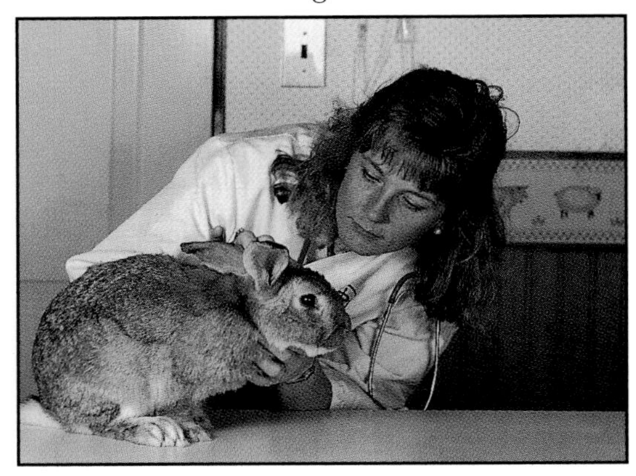

The best way to find a rabbit vet is by referral. Ask other rabbit owners who they use, and whether they are happy with this individual or clinic. Speak to the breeder or rescuer from whom you got your rabbit. If you don't know any other rabbit owners near you, contact the House Rabbit Society. (See Chapter

12.) People there will be able to help you locate a rabbit vet in your area.

Once you have selected a veterinarian, it's a good idea to take your new rabbit in for an examination. The veterinarian will be able to tell you if your pet has any potential health problems and will set up an appointment for a spay or neuter. This will also give you an opportunity to meet the doctor and start a file on your rabbit. Should you find yourself in an emergency later on, you will already have established a relationship with your vet. This is also a good time to ask your vet to show you how to clip your rabbit's nails and answer any questions you may have on how to care for your new pet.

Keep an eye out to make sure your rabbit doesn't come into contact with hazardous substances.

Observation

Get to know your rabbit and keep a close eye on him. If you know how he looks when he is healthy, you'll be more likely to recognize signs of illness early on. Many diseases that can be fatal are often curable in their earliest stages. Realizing your rabbit is "under the weather" before he becomes seriously ill could be the key to his recovery.

Regular grooming is an important part of observation, since this hands-on procedure will encourage you to take a close look at your pet. The tasks required during regular grooming, such as maintenance of your pet's nails and regular brushing, are essential to prevent illness and injury.

Examine your rabbit's litter box regularly. Keep an eye out for diarrhea, lack of feces or passed hairballs—all of which can indicate a possible problem.

If your rabbit exhibits any of these signs, contact your veterinarian immediately.

Spaying/Neutering

One of the leading causes of death in older female rabbits is uterine cancer. You can prevent this illness in your doe by having her spayed after the age of four months. Spaying, a removal of the internal female organs, also prevents breast cancer and other hormone-related illnesses.

If your rabbit is a male, neutering (removal of the testes) after the age of four months can help him stay healthy, as well. Unneutered male rabbits often become aggressive and frequently get injured in fights with rabbits and other pets. Males who have not been neutered often spray urine as a territorial marker, creating odorous messes for their owners to clean. Since neutering is a simple veterinary procedure, it is well worth the effort.

SIGNS OF ILL HEALTH

How will you know if your rabbit isn't feeling well? In addition to drastic changes in behavior, here are some telltale signs to watch for:

- a dull look in the eyes,
- lethargy,
- loud teeth grinding,
- loss of appetite,
- constipation/diarrhea,
- discharge from eyes or nose,
- bloated abdomen,
- labored breathing,
- unexplained weight loss.

Common Ailments

There are quite a few illnesses that affect rabbits, but many are rarely seen. Below is a list of the most common health problems in pet rabbits today.

Abscesses

Abscesses are bacterial infections that result from a puncture wound of some kind. If your rabbit has cut himself on something or has had a fight with another pet, he may develop an abscess at the site of the injury.

You will recognize an abscess by its round appearance and the discharge and foul smell that usually accompany it. Your veterinarian will treat your rabbit with antibiotics to rid him of the infection.

Coccidiosis

A very common illness in rabbits, coccidiosis is caused by protozoa that affect the digestive system. Symptoms include loss of appetite, diarrhea, poor coat, distended abdomen and weight loss. Coccidiosis is most often seen in rabbits that are kept in unsanitary cages. Since this disease is almost always fatal, it's important to keep your rabbit's cage as clean as possible.

Constipation/Diarrhea

Difficulty defecating (constipation) or a very loose stool (diarrhea) can be the result of either poor diet or illness. Symptoms that usually indicate constipation are straining during elimination, lack of feces in the litter box, distended abdomen and lethargy. Diarrhea is usually indicated by a loose or runny stool and a dirty tail. If you see evidence that your rabbit is experiencing either of these problems, take him to your veterinarian to have the problem assessed.

Fleas

The same fleas that attack dogs and cats also prey on rabbits. You'll know if your rabbit is plagued by a flea infestation if you find dark spots that resemble particles of black dirt in its fur. To verify that a particle is "flea dirt," place it on a paper towel and put a drop of water on it. If it turns red, then the particle is digested blood left on your pet by a flea. If your rabbit has light-colored fur, you may even see a few of these tiny pests hopping around on your animal's body.

Fleas can be treated in several different ways. The most effective method is to apply a rabbit-safe chemical to the pet while also applying another spray to the rabbit's environment. Your veterinarian can supply you with the proper products as well as detailed instructions on how to rid your rabbit of these pests.

FLIES

Flies can be very dangerous to rabbits, particularly to those kept outdoors. They often lay their eggs on a rabbit's soiled rectal area, leaving maggots to burrow in and feed on the animal's flesh. Flies can be kept at bay by keeping both your rabbit's cage and his fur clean. If flies do lay eggs on your rabbit, contact a veterinarian for assistance.

Drinking pineapple juice can be helpful to a rabbit with hairball problems.

HAIRBALLS

Because rabbits are such voracious groomers, they frequently ingest large volumes of their own hair. Since rabbits cannot vomit, they must pass any hair they swallow. If a rabbit is not getting enough roughage in his diet, this hair can cause intestinal blockages and eventual death. Signs of a hairball problem include loss of appetite and masses of hair in the feces. Giving your rabbit a small amount of pineapple juice every month or so can help him with this problem, but it is a preventative measure, not a cure. Consult your veterinarian with any noticeable problem.

Heat Prostration

Rabbits are very susceptible to overheating. When the weather is hot, keep a close eye on your pet. Signs of heat prostration include a stretched out posture, panting, rapid breathing and foaming at the mouth. If you find your rabbit in this state, move him to a cool place out of the sun and place a cold, wet towel around his head. Offer him some fresh water. Heat prostration constitutes an emergency situation. Contact your veterinarian immediately.

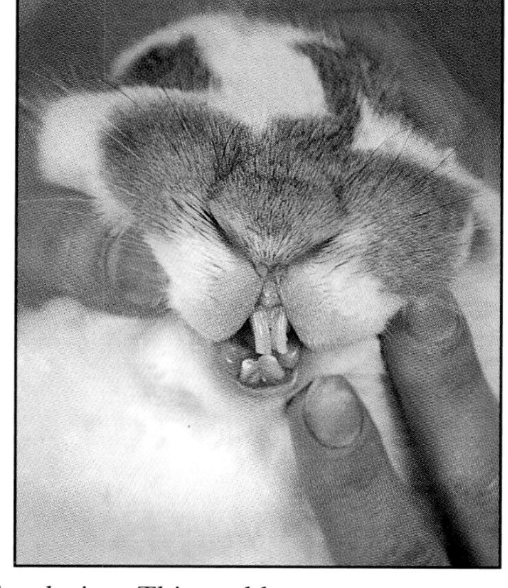

Misaligned teeth on a rabbit present quite a problem; they must be trimmed regularly by a veterinarian.

Malocclusion

When a rabbit's front teeth do not wear down properly, the condition is known as malocclusion. This problem is usually genetic, the result of teeth that are misaligned. Signs of malocclusion include overly long teeth, infections in the mouth, ulcerations on the lips or tongue, jaw problems and difficulty eating. This is a common problem in rabbits, and must be handled by a veterinarian to prevent eventual death. Treatment consists of either regular trimming or complete removal of the teeth.

Mites

Rabbits are susceptible to two different kinds of mites: fur mites and ear mites. **Fur mites** cause patches of skin on the rabbit's body to become red and scabby. Clumps of hair are often missing. **Ear mites** settle in the rabbit's ear canals, causing itching and a dark, waxy discharge. Both of these mites are easily spread from one animal to another. Contact your veterinarian for information on how to treat either of these parasites.

Myxomatosis

Myxomatosis is a sort of rabbit plague. Spread deliberately throughout Europe in the 1800s to kill off large populations of wild rabbits, the disease still exists today. Mostly found in coastal California and Oregon, myxomatosis causes swelling around the eyelids, ears and nose, and a high fever. Nearly always fatal, this virus is spread by mosquitoes and biting flies. If you live in an area where myxomatosis is common in wild rabbit populations, it might be wise to keep your pet indoors.

Skin and ear mites can be quite unpleasant; keep your rabbit's ears clean and check them often to prevent an infestation.

Obesity

Veterinarians report that obesity is the biggest health problem they see in rabbits. Rabbits who are overweight are prone to a number of illnesses that affect major organs. The primary cause of obesity in rabbits is the overfeeding of pellets. Rabbits who are obese should be placed on a special diet to help them get down to their proper weight.

Pastuerellosis

Also known as "snuffles," this common bacterial disease affects the rabbit's respiratory system. Characterized by sneezing and coughing, along with wet and matted fur on the front legs, pastuerellosis is highly contagious and should be treated with antibiotics.

Ringworm

This fungus, which also affects humans, cats, dogs, horses and other animals, causes dandruff and fur loss on rabbits. Since it is highly contagious, immediate treatment by a veterinarian is recommended.

Sore Hocks

Rabbits who live in cages with wire floors often develop sore hocks. This condition is typified by red, swollen skin on the hind legs with accompanying hair loss. A veterinarian will provide an antibiotic ointment for treatment and will recommend a change in cage flooring.

Wet Dewlap

When a rabbit repeatedly dips his head into a bowl of water, a condition called wet dewlap can result. Infection often occurs in the dewlap, chin and front legs since the skin in these areas is nearly always wet. Does are especially prone to this disease, since their dewlaps are considerably larger than those of bucks.

Wet dewlap should be treated by a veterinarian, who will prescribe either an antibacterial or antifungal ointment, depending on the nature of the infection. This ailment can be prevented with the use of a gravity water bottle instead of a water bowl.

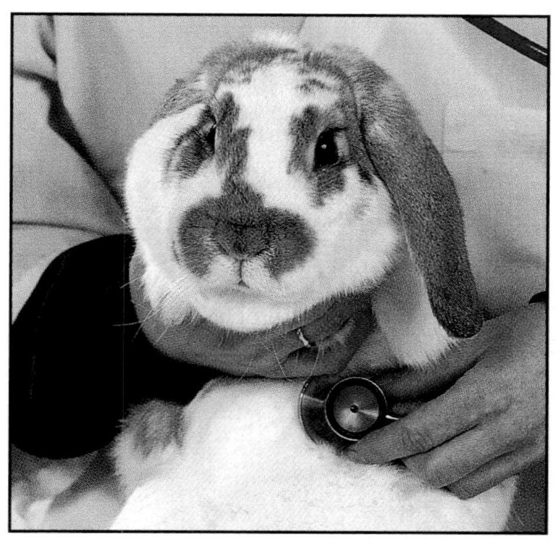

Close observation by you and regular check-up by a vet will ensure your rabbit's good health.

Worms

Roundworms and **tapeworms,** two parasites that commonly afflict dogs, also prey on rabbits. Symptoms of worm infestation include a distended abdomen, poor coat condition and worms in the litter box or near the anus. To prevent your rabbit from contracting these parasites, keep him away from outdoor areas where dogs defecate. If you suspect that your rabbit has worms, contact your veterinarian.

Enjoying
your

part three

Rabbit

chapter 9

Understanding Your Rabbit

In order to have a rewarding relationship with your rabbit, it's important that you understand her. The domestic rabbit is very similar to the wild rabbit in the way that she behaves and communicates. The instincts you see expressed by your pet mimic those of rabbits in nature.

Rabbit Behavior

To understand rabbit behavior, you must first realize that rabbits are prey animals. In the wild, they live their entire lives on the lookout for larger animals who want to eat them. Each individual rabbit's ability to be alert, wary and quick is what keeps her alive.

Protective Instincts in the Wild

Wild rabbits have a number of behaviors that help them avoid predators. In fact, every behavior that rabbits possess is designed to help them survive in the wild. The habit of standing on hind legs is one of these behaviors. Rabbits use this posture to take in their surroundings and judge the safety of their whereabouts. A rabbit standing on her hind legs will use her sense of sight, hearing and smell to check out the neighborhood to see if any predators are lurking nearby.

The old adage "safety in numbers" applies to the wild rabbit, who lives in social groups known as **colonies** that can contain as many as fifteen individual rabbits. Life in a group provides the rabbit with security on a couple of levels. First, the more rabbits there are, the safer it is for each individual rabbit. For every rabbit who lives in the colony, there is another set of eyes scouring the landscape, on the lookout for enemies. When one rabbit spies a predator, she gives a signal to the others that danger is near.

Rabbits access a number of self-defense mechanisms when threatened, including hunching down close to the ground and remaining perfectly still.

The **warren,** a complex set of underground burrows created by the colony, provides another form of protection against predators. Since warrens consist of many different burrows, there are rarely a shortage of holes to dive into when an enemy approaches.

Another way that wild rabbits protect themselves from predators is to freeze and flatten their bodies against the ground. If you have ever come across a wild rabbit on a nature trail or in a park, you may have noticed that the animal stopped in its tracks once it saw you and stayed there, motionless, in a flushed position. While human eyes are keen to the differences in color between a rabbit and a background of shrubs or grass, most predators cannot make the distinction. To a coyote or bobcat, the rabbit's agouti fur blends right into the foliage. This game of camouflage works well for the rabbit, who often goes unseen.

LITTLE-KNOWN RABBIT FACTS

Did you know that your rabbit . . .

- can be trained?
- can be taught to use a litter box?
- can purr with her teeth?
- can be trained to walk on leash?
- has constantly growing teeth?
- can jump up to three feet high?
- can be highly affectionate and loyal?
- will sometimes get the notion to play a game of tag with you?

In the event that the camouflage doesn't work and the predator does attack, the rabbit is equipped with strong hindquarters to help her dash away. Sprinters by design, rabbits can reach speeds of up to twenty-four miles per hour over a short distance. They use this swiftness to get their lithe bodies to a hole or other place where they can hide.

Rabbit Social Hierarchy

In addition to their self-protection instincts, rabbits also live by a set of instinctual behaviors that allow them to live peacefully within their communities. Each rabbit colony contains a dominant male and a dominant female, with the other members of the group assuming various levels of dominance and submission below them. This social hierarchy contributes to the survival of the species; the strongest, most dominant animals are likely to outlive the lesser members of the colony and go on to reproduce.

The dominant male in the colony eats the best food, and the dominant female gets to raise her young in the main warren. Other females who are less important in status have to raise their kits in burrows that are separate from the main group. This arrangement ensures that the offspring of the strongest, most able animals will survive to adulthood.

Despite these differences in rank among individuals, the colony of rabbits works as a group to protect its territory from other intruding rabbits. Wild rabbits rarely venture far from the safety of the warren, and establish territories that they consider their own. Marking of this territory and fighting is common among wild rabbits, who must prevent other rabbits from encroaching upon their turf.

Communicating with Your Rabbit

Your pet rabbit has not changed very much since her species was domesticated several hundred years ago. The same instincts expressed by her ancestors live on in her genes.

In order to communicate with your rabbit and develop a good relationship with her, you need to understand how these instincts translate into behaviors displayed within the domestic environment you have created for your pet.

Easing Fears

Always remember that rabbits are prey animals and are easily frightened. When you sense that your rabbit is afraid, speak to her in a soft voice and move slowly around her. This will help your rabbit distinguish you from an attacking predator, who would move quickly and aggressively.

Your rabbit may appear to be afraid of something or someone that you consider harmless. Try to put yourself in your rabbit's position. Since she does not have the power to reason that we humans do, she is not able to understand why she shouldn't be afraid of something that, while seemingly innocuous to us, appears threatening to her.

Be Considerate and Consistent

Know, too, that your rabbit's ears are very sensitive. Designed to be able to detect the sounds of lurking predators, they are especially sensitive to the loud noises of a human environment. For this reason, noise should be kept to an absolute minimum. The kindest thing a rabbit owner can do is to create a quiet, soothing atmosphere for his or her pet.

Rabbits in the wild forage for food mostly in the early morning hours and during twilight. They create a regular schedule for themselves and stick to it. Given this, the most natural time for your rabbit to eat is in the morning and evening. Be consistent with your pet, providing her with her breakfast and dinner at the same time every day.

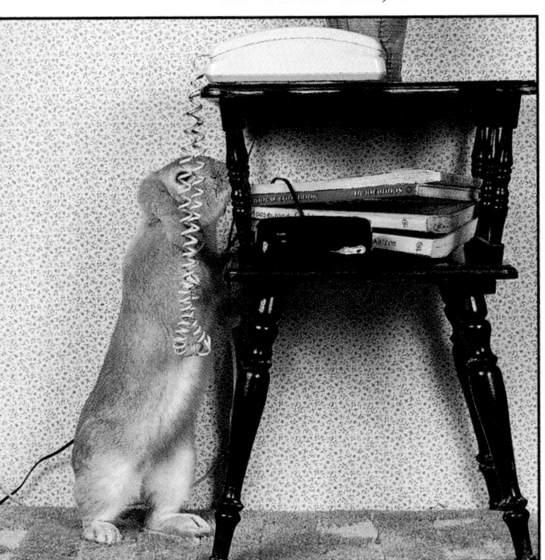

Once a rabbit feels comfortable in her surroundings, her curious nature will soon become evident.

Keep in mind that young rabbits are different from older rabbits in their behavior and attitudes. Rabbits under a year old have not reached their full maturity. This means they will often behave in a rambunctious manner, much like a puppy or kitten. Young rabbits tend to be particularly active when it comes to chewing, spraying and digging. Neutering or spaying can help, as can a lot of tolerance and understanding on your part. Patience is the key to helping a rabbit get through this "teenage" period. A more mature and less troublesome adult will undoubtedly emerge with the passage of time.

Body Language

As you spend time with your rabbit, you will begin to notice that she has certain mannerisms and actions that may seem odd to you. Because rabbits communicate primarily with body language, most of the behaviors you witness are silent messages about how your rabbit feels about you and her environment.

Rabbits mark their territory by rubbing the scent glands on their chins on any handy object.

Chin Rubbing If you have ever noticed your rabbit rubbing her chin on the corners of the furniture, the edges of her nestbox, or on your hand, you are witnessing a display of territorial marking. The scent glands located on the underside of your rabbit's face leave an odor detectable to other rabbits. When another rabbit smells the odor, it will know that this particular territory belongs to the owner of that scent. A rabbit feels safest in territory she has marked.

Ear Shaking Many rabbits use their ears to express their dislike for something. If your rabbit smells something unpleasant or does not want to be handled anymore, she may shake her ears in an attempt to rid herself of whatever is annoying her. This is a cue to you that your rabbit is displeased

Flattening Wild rabbits flatten their bodies to avoid being seen by predators, as do pet rabbits. If your rabbit is nervous when approached by strangers or other pets, you may see her lower herself to the ground, with her ears held tightly against her head and her eyes bulging from their sockets. This stance is one of fear. If your rabbit assumes this position, reassure her that everything is okay and remove her from the situation that is frightening her.

Kicking Rabbits engage in different types of kicking, depending on what kind of mood they're in. When a rabbit is being held incorrectly or feels insecure because of the way she is being lifted, she will kick ferociously in an effort to escape. Kicking is also used in play, especially by rabbits who are joyously running about.

Licking Rabbits lick for much the same reason that cats or dogs do: to show affection. Rabbits will groom one another with their tongues and will also "groom" their human friends as well. If your rabbit licks you, she is trying to tell you that she thinks you are special.

Lying Down When your rabbit is tired and wants to sleep, she will lay on her side with her legs extended. You may even see your rabbit lie on her abdomen with her legs stretched out behind her! A rabbit in this position is resting and should not be disturbed.

Once you begin to understand your rabbit's body language, you'll be better able to understand what she's thinking.

Sounds While rabbits are primarily silent creatures, they do vocalize on occasion. A rabbit will **hiss** when she is feeling aggressive, usually toward another rabbit. **Purring** is a noise rabbits make when they are contented, although it is different from a cat's purr. The sound of a rabbit's purr is created by her teeth. **Clicking** is a sound made by some rabbits after they eat something particularly tasty. **Soft teeth grinding** is a sound made by a happy rabbit, while **loud teeth grinding** is a sign of severe pain. **Screaming** is something rabbits do only when they are very frightened, usually when they are being attacked by a predator.

Squatting Not to be confused with flattening, this posture is a relaxed one. Your rabbit will appear to be squatting down with her ears folded gently against her head. She will not have the frightened look in her eye that accompanies the flattening position and instead will appear comfortable and at ease.

Thumping In the movie *Bambi,* a little gray rabbit named Thumper got his name by repeatedly stamping his back leg on the ground. This behavior is not just the stuff cartoons are made of. Real-life rabbits actually thump their hind legs on the ground whenever they want to issue a warning of some kind. You may see your rabbit do this under a variety of circumstances, usually when something has attracted her attention and made her uncertain.

chapter 10

Fun with Bunny

While many people think rabbits are boring creatures who do nothing but sit in a cage all day, those who live closely with rabbits know that this assumption is wrong.

Rabbits have gained a reputation in the past as uninteresting animals because, until recently, they were primarily kept as outdoor pets and received little human contact. Nowadays, however, many people have begun keeping their rabbits inside the house where the animals can interact with people and other pets. Even many outdoor rabbits now get to spend some time indoors, roaming through the house and joining in the day's activities with their humans.

Given the rabbit's newfound opportunity to show us what he's all about, it's not surprising that people are discovering what a unique and fascinating pet he really is.

Playing

In the wild, rabbits are playful creatures who love to engage their fellow rabbits in games. R.M. Lockley, researcher and author of *The Private Life of the Rabbit,* observed wild rabbits chasing each other, running in circles, jumping into the air and rolling in the grass. In the situations Lockley observed, there was no other reason for this behavior than the fact that the rabbits felt good and wanted to show it.

Much like their wild ancestors, pet rabbits also like to play. Rabbits have been known to play with dogs and cats, as well as with other rabbits. They're even likely to play with humans if the game is right. Rabbits also love to amuse themselves with toys.

Despite what many people think, rabbits can actually be quite playful creatures.

When it comes to interactive play with a rabbit, the decision on which game to play is best left up to the rabbit. Rabbits have been know to initiate games of tag with humans, to play "bat the ball" and to chase toys being dragged around in a circle. Because of their wary nature, a game of chase initiated by a human will usually frighten a rabbit, who may suddenly feel like it is being preyed upon. However, if your rabbit starts to chase you, he either wants you to leave the area, or he is trying to play tag with you!

The best way to enjoy a rabbit at play is to give him a toy and then sit back and watch. Rabbits love to frolic around with a favorite toy, and their antics can be quite amusing. Playtime is beneficial for them too, both physically and emotionally.

Toys

There are a number of toys you can provide for your rabbit. Store-bought toys made especially for rabbits are usually made from wood and can be batted about and then chewed on for hours. You can also amuse your rabbit with more readily available cat toys, including small rubber balls, plastic balls with bells in them and stuffed socks. If you do decide to offer your rabbit such toys, just be sure not to let him chew them. Swallowing a piece of plastic or fabric can be harmful to a rabbit.

A simple paper bag can provide hours of fun for your rabbit.

There are a number of household items that make excellent toys for rabbits. Try offering your pet a paper cup, an empty soda can, a small towel, a toilet paper spool, a cardboard box, straw baskets, a can with a penny or stone inside of it or a paper grocery bag. Alternate your rabbit's toys so he doesn't get bored with them.

Traveling

If you go on a trip to the beach, can you bring your rabbit with you? What if you are going to visit a relative a few hours away? The answer to these questions is either yes or no, depending on your rabbit and how you plan to get there.

If you want to travel with your pet, make sure you take along the necessary supplies.

Since new situations often cause stress and anxiety in rabbits, and since new environments can mean exposure to disease and parasites, it's usually best to leave your pet at home while traveling. Ask a knowledgeable friend to take care of the rabbit, or hire a professional pet sitter to care for him while you're gone.

While some rabbits do not respond well to traveling, others enjoy the chance to get out of the house once in a while. If you take the proper precautions, you should be able to give your pet a change of scenery while still keeping him healthy.

Traveling by Airplane

Airplane rides are not recommended for rabbits unless absolutely necessary. If you are planning to fly somewhere, your rabbit would be better off left at home. Airplane travel is difficult for rabbits since most pets must travel in the plane's cargo hold, where temperatures are not often controlled. Pets frequently die of heatstroke while a plane sits on the runway waiting to

take off, or from cold while the plane is high in the atmosphere.

While some airlines do allow pets in the cabin of the aircraft, they must be kept in a pet carrier and placed underneath the seat in front of yours. Only very small rabbits will fit in these carriers, and even those rarely do so comfortably. All in all, the benefits of bringing your rabbit along on your vacation are probably not great enough to justify the stress your pet will encounter while traveling by air.

Fitting your rabbit with a harness and leash will make travel of all sorts with your rabbit an easier and more exciting adventure.

Traveling by Car

Rabbits can ride comfortably in cars when the day is cool and the traffic is minimal. If you must spend a significant amount of time sitting in traffic, try to keep the windows rolled up. Rabbits are sensitive to car exhaust.

If you want to find out if your rabbit is the adventurous type who enjoys travel, you'll first need to get him used to the idea of riding in the car and being out of his usual surroundings.

Start by leaving his travel carrier in a place where he can have as much access to it as possible. Since rabbits feel most secure in small enclosures, you'll find that your rabbit will like to spend time in his carrier. Placing some hay in it as well will encourage him to visit the carrier often.

Using a Harness and Leash

In the meantime, work on getting him used to wearing a harness and walking on a leash. Begin by putting his harness on him and letting him hop around the house under supervision. Once he seems at ease wearing the harness, you can then snap a leash on it and walk around the house with him.

Keep in mind that you will not be able to walk your rabbit in the same way that you would walk a dog. Rabbits cannot be taught to walk beside you or do most of the other things that leash-trained dogs do. Instead, your rabbit will hop around, and you will basically follow him. Remember to always be gentle with your rabbit while walking him. If you need to get from one place to another while he is on the leash, pick him up and carry him there.

Believe it or not, rabbits can be trained to walk—or hop—on a leash.

When your rabbit is comfortably walking on his harness, try taking him outdoors with it. Let him explore your backyard or another safe area, taking care not to allow him to eat any unknown plants or walk through areas that may have been sprayed with pesticides or visited by dogs.

Eventually, you'll be able to walk your rabbit out on the street or in a nearby park. Remember that your pet is vulnerable when he is outside of his home. It's up to you to keep an eye out for loose dogs who would love nothing more than to have a good rouse with your bunny. Be sure to never leave your rabbit unattended or tied to anything, since he could become tangled in his leash and might panic. You will notice that your "rabbit on a leash" will get you a lot of attention from passers-by and will be the subject of many impromptu conversations.

Once your rabbit seems at ease with both the carrier and the harness, you can start preparing for outings by taking him for short rides in the car. Start by taking short, twenty-minute drives and then gradually lengthen your trips. If your rabbit is the traveling type, he will eventually get used to the routine and will settle down and relax.

Once your rabbit feels okay about riding in the car, you can try taking him on a short trip and then walking him in his harness once you arrive at your destination. If your rabbit seems comfortable and is enjoying his adventure, then you may have a real traveler on your hands. He may be the type of rabbit you can take with you when you go to visit friends or spend a day picnicking in the park.

Bring Along a Bit of Home

Remember to bring along some of your rabbit's necessities. A supply of his regular food is a must, as is fresh hay, which should be placed in his carrier for him to munch on. His water bottle and a jug of the water you usually give him are also necessary. (Providing him with familiar water will ensure that he drinks as much as he needs.) Be sure to bring his litter box, too, so he can use it once you arrive at your destination. Try to adhere to your normal schedule of feeding so as not to disrupt your rabbit's system.

Showing

Quite a few people who start out as casual pet owners eventually start showing their rabbits. Showing is a fun activity in which the entire family can participate. People who begin by simply showing a pet often become heavily involved in the activity and end up acquiring a number of rabbits.

If you and your family want to investigate the world of rabbit shows, you may first want to look into 4-H, an organization created to help children learn how to care for and exhibit livestock. The American Rabbit Breeders Association (ARBA), the official organization for rabbit showing, is another group that sponsors rabbit shows around the country. These shows are attended by rabbit fanciers who take the sport of showing quite seriously.

4-H

4-H, which is short for "head, heart, hands and health," was started in the early part of the twentieth century by a community of farmers who wanted to encourage the development of agrarian skills in children. In 1907, it officially became part of the U.S. Department of Agriculture (USDA).

Since then, the 4-H youth program has grown to be a large national network of local clubs, featuring projects that range from cattle to computers. Rabbits have long been a part of 4-H and have proven to be a very popular project over the past several decades. 4-H is an excellent way for young rabbit owners to learn to show rabbits and care for them.

Joining a 4-H rabbit project will help your child learn how to care for and handle rabbits.

Shows specifically for 4-H rabbit owners are held around the country. These shows follow the rules and breed standards established by ARBA. 4-H members can also exhibit their rabbits at county fairs, since 4-H often has a strong presence at these events.

The mission of 4-H as a whole is to promote the farming way of life and to help young people develop their potential to learn. There are 4-H clubs around the country, managed by the nation's land-grant universities. General guidelines are established by the USDA, and individual states follow these rules while establishing their own regulations for clubs in their jurisdictions. The Cooperative

Extension Services in each state administers the state's 4-H clubs.

Open to children aged nine to nineteen (and sometimes even younger, depending on the individual club), typical 4-H rabbit projects feature hands-on learning in a family environment. Children are taught how to feed, care for, handle, groom and show their rabbits.

4-H Clubs are run by volunteers, usually parents whose children have been involved with the program for some time. Individual 4-H projects, such as rabbits, have leaders as well. These people are usually parents, and tend to be breeders or former breeders who have spent a substantial amount of time showing rabbits.

Owning purebred rabbits, like these Mini Rexes, can lead to a rewarding involvement in rabbit showing.

Aside from valuable learning and hands-on experience, members of 4-H rabbit projects can also earn awards. While these vary from club to club, typical activities, such as displaying a winning rabbit-related project in the local 4-H fair, or successfully exhibiting a rabbit at a show, can earn participants medals, ribbons or certificates.

If your child has a rabbit that is not a purebred, he or she can still show the animal in 4-H under the showmanship class. In showmanship, the exhibitor presents the rabbit to a judge, demonstrating a knowledge of rabbit care and anatomy as well as proper handling. Children are graded on their ability to present the animal properly and to understand their pet's overall health. The rules followed for showmanship classes are established by ARBA, which also offers these classes.

To obtain information on a local 4-H rabbit project, contact your county extension office (usually listed in the telephone directory). For general information about 4-H, contact the National 4-H Council listed in Chapter 12.

ARBA

The American Rabbit Breeders Association, which began in the early part of the twentieth century, is the governing body for rabbit showing and registration in the United States. ARBA sanctions rabbit shows around the country. These shows, put on by regional rabbit clubs, can sometimes be open to only one breed, but are often open to all breeds of rabbits.

Nothing is quite as rewarding as the love and affection of a cherished pet rabbit.

ARBA has created a list of rules and regulations for rabbit shows, and each sanctioned show operates by these rules. Judges who officiate at ARBA shows evaluate the rabbits they judge using the breed standards published by ARBA. Rabbits that are exhibited at ARBA shows may be registered with the organization (more information on how to register follows in this chapter), but doing so is not mandatory.

Rabbits at ARBA shows are judged in classes organized by breed. Within the breed classification, rabbits are then divided by age before they are judged. Awards are

given to individual class winners, as well as Best of Breed, Best of Opposite Sex (given to the best rabbit of the sex opposite the Best of Breed winner), Best of Variety or Group and ultimately, Best in Show. Class winners usually receive a ribbon; Best of Variety or Group, a rosette; Best of Breed, a trophy; and Best in Show, a large trophy. Small cash awards are also given to some of the winners.

When competing in ARBA shows, rabbits can earn "legs" toward their Grand Championship. Three legs qualify a rabbit as a Grand Champion, which is a distinctive title in the rabbit world.

Registration It is not necessary to register a rabbit in order to show it. However, many people choose to do so since having a registered rabbit assures that the animal's pedigree is true and that the rabbit meets all the requirements of its breed.

In order to register a rabbit in the purebred classification, the animal needs a three-generation pedigree. The rabbit must be examined by an official ARBA registrar, who will determine if the rabbit is eligible for registration. The rabbit must be six months or older and meet the senior weight limits for its breed. It must also be free from disqualifications or eliminations as defined by its breed standard.

In order to register a rabbit, you, as the rabbit's owner, must be a member of ARBA. You will also have to pay a fee for registering your animal.

ARBA registrars are present at ARBA-sanctioned shows. To have your rabbit registered, you must bring the rabbit and its papers to the show, or make arrangements with a registrar to see the rabbit at the registrar's home. It takes about three weeks to receive your registration papers in the mail once the examination process is complete.

Tattoos If you go to a rabbit show, you will notice that some rabbits have tattoos on the inside of one ear. In order for a rabbit to be shown at an ARBA show, it must be tattooed with an identification number, usually the rabbit's registration number. Tattooing is frequently done when the registrar first examines and assigns a registration number to the rabbit. You may also see an ARBA registrar actually tattooing rabbits at a show. Some breeders do their own tattooing, using a system of letters and numbers that they have created for their own record-keeping purposes.

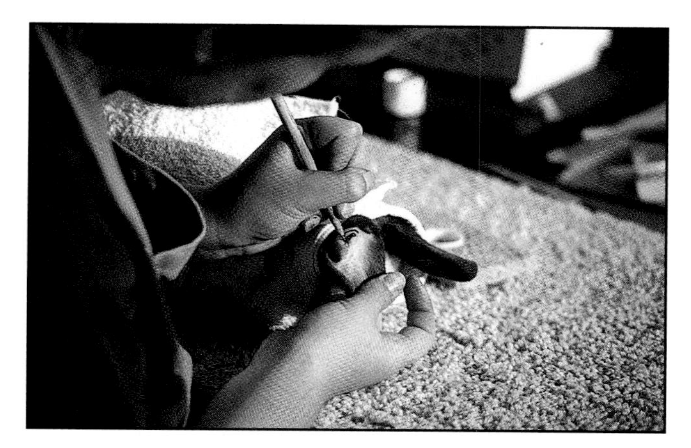

Some rabbits are tattooed right at the show site.

Some people opt not to show their pets since they do not wish to tattoo their animals. A tattoo leaves a permanent mark on the rabbit's ear, and the process causes pain, albeit brief, to the rabbit. Another downside to showing your pet is the pressure it causes the rabbit to feel. Showing can be stressful for any animal, and rabbits are no exception. Your rabbit's chances of contracting a contagious disease will be greater if you show him, since he will be exposed to a large number of other rabbits. For these reasons and others, many rabbit owners choose not to exhibit their pets.

Regardless of whether you decide to show your rabbit, you will undoubtedly get countless hours of joy from your new pet. Your dedicated and concerned care will be returned to you in the form of your rabbit's faithful love and affection.

part four

Beyond the Basics

chapter 11

Resources

Books

Adams, Richard George. *Watership Down.* New York: Scribner, 1996.

Bennett, Bob. *Storey's Guide to Raising Rabbits.* Pownal, Vermont: Storey Publishing, 2000.

Harriman, Marinell. *House Rabbit Handbook: How to Live with an Urban Rabbit.* Alameda, California: Drollery Press, 1995.

Fraser, Samantha, and Samantha Hunter. *Hop to It: A Guide to Training Your Pet Rabbit.* Hauppauge, New York: Barron's Educational Series, 1991.

Kanable, Ann. *Raising Rabbits.* Emmaus, Pennsylvania: Rodale Press, 1981.

McNitt, J.I. *Rabbit Production.* Danville, Illinois: Interstate Publishing, 2000.

Potter, Beatrix. *The Complete Tales of Peter Rabbit and Other Favorite Stories.* Philadelphia: Courage Books, 1991.

Wegler, Monika. *Dwarf Rabbits.* Hauppauge, New York: Barron's Educational Series, 1998.

Magazines

House Rabbit Journal
To receive the journal you must join the House Rabbit Society. Contact them at:
148 Broadway
Richmond, CA 94804
(510) 970-7575
www.rabbit.org/journal/index.html

Rabbit Gazette
R. G. Publishing
1725 SW Boulevard
Kansas City, KS 66103
(913) 722-2229

Rabbits Only
P.O. Box 207
Holbrook, NY 11741
(516) 737-0763
E-mail: info@rabbits.com
www.rabbits.com

Videos

The Geisha Boy
This 1958 film stars Jerry Lewis and a New Zealand White Rabbit.

Rabbits
Pocket Pet Series
If you want to sit back, relax and learn all about your lagomorph, order this handy video. You'll find everything from how to prepare your home for a pet rabbit, to how to select the perfect bunny for you. To order, contact:
S.E.I. Distribution
Pierce-Arrow Productions, Inc.
P.O. Box 6663
Los Osos, CA 93402
E-mail: info@pocket-pet-series.com
www.pocket-pet-series.com

Watership Down
The film adaptation of Richard Adams' bestseller was made in 1978 and features a group of (cartoon) rabbits searching for a new place to live after their warren is destroyed.

Who Framed Roger Rabbit?
Featuring Bob Hoskins and the curvaceously animated Jessica Rabbit (Kathleen Turner), this 1988 film is sure to appeal to audiences of all ages.

Web Sites

House Rabbit Society
www.rabbit.org

The House Rabbit Society is the premier organization for folks who keep rabbits as house pets. This site offers plenty of tips on rabbit care, along with links to the newly opened House Rabbit Society Adoption Center and the organization's newsletter, *The House Rabbit Society Journal.*

American Rabbit Breeders Association (ARBA)
www.nmia.com/~arba/index.htm

The ARBA is dedicated to exhibiting and judging show rabbits. Membership in the organization entitles you to a subscription to *Domestic Rabbits Magazine* along with other privileges.

Friends of Rabbits
www.friendsofrabbits.org

This online organization devotes itself to rescuing homeless and abandoned domestic rabbits. Friends of Rabbits also promotes proper rabbit care through educational articles and advice that is posted on its Web site.

Rabbits Online
www.rabbitsonline.com

This colorful site offers bite-sized morsels of information on everything bunny related. Whether you are interested in viewing photographs of rabbits or in discovering the optimal dimensions of a rabbit hutch, this is the place to visit.

Bunny Luv
www.bunnyluv.com

This is the perfect place to shop for the special rabbit in your life. Whether you're looking for a customized toy for your lagomorph to play with, or some organic apple wood for him to chew on, you are sure to find it at Bunny Luv.

Rabbits, Rabbits, Rabbits
http://jan.ucc.nau.edu/~julie/buns/bun.html

For an all-around online resource, be sure to visit Rabbits, Rabbits, Rabbits. This Web site offers sample articles from *The Bunny Thymes* newsletter, links to reputable rabbit breeders, information on lagomorphic medical concerns and fun stuff—T-shirts, jewelry and more—featuring rabbits.

Rabbit Web
www.rabbitweb.net

This Web site offers plenty of information on every aspect of rabbit keeping and raising. Visit to read about common health concerns in rabbits, discover exactly what breed your bunny is or find out how to litter train your pet.

Clubs

In many areas, rabbit enthusiasts have formed clubs and associations where lagomorph-raising techniques can be shared. Listed below is a sampling of national rabbit breed clubs and organizations.

National Associations

House Rabbit Society
148 Broadway
Richmond, CA 94804
(510) 970-7575
www.rabbit.org

Membership includes a subscription to the *House Rabbit Journal.* Send a self-addressed, stamped envelope to the above address for more information.

American Rabbit Breeders Association (ARBA)
P.O. Box 426
Bloomington, IL 61702
(309) 664-7500
E-mail: arbapost@aol.com

Official governing body for rabbit shows in the United States.

National 4-H Council
7100 Connecticut Avenue
Chevy Chase, MD 20815
(301) 961-2840
www.fourhcouncil.edu/index.htm

Can provide general information on 4-H.

Rabbit Breed Clubs

American Belgian Hare Club
62 West Main Street
Upton, MA 01568
(508) 529-6495
http://members.tripod.com/~aliene22/belharerabbit.htm

American Beveren Rabbit Club
5830 West County Road 550N
Mulberry, IN 46058-9779
(765) 296-3558
www.showbunny.com/beveren.asp

American Blue & White Rabbit Club
40 Wilsey Road
Greenfield Center, NY 12833
(518) 885-3590

American Britannia Petite Rabbit Society
Ron Rohrig, Sanction Secretary
P.O. Box 2651
Richmond, IN 47375
(765) 966-8686
E-mail: RonRohrig@aol.com

American Checkered Giant Rabbit Club, Inc.
542 Aspen Street NW
Toledo, OR 97391
(541) 336-2543
E-mail: EDWARDS@fbo.com

American Chinchilla Rabbit Breeders Association
1529 9th Street North
Fargo, ND 58102-2207
(701) 237-3034

American Dutch Rabbit Club, Inc.
Route 1, Box 95
Lewiston, MN 55952
(507) 864-2103
E-mail: dbengt@rushford.polaristel.net

American Dwarf Hotot Rabbit Club
68 Clover Court
Granville, OH 43023
(740) 587-2231
E-mail: blarimer@gurulink.com

American English Spot Rabbit Club
513 East Kent Road
Lubbock, TX 79403
(806) 762-1918
E-mail: berrypatch@worldnet.att.net

American Federation of New Zealand Rabbit Breeders
23628 South Highway 211
Colton, OR 97017
(503) 630-6193
E-mail: Haybox@aol.com

American Fuzzy Lop Rabbit Club
Pat Vezino, Sanction Secretary
P.O. Box 65
Sunfield, MI 48890
(517) 566-8218
E-mail: sdrabbitry@voyager.net

American Harlequin Rabbit Club
1299 Josie Lane
Conover, NC 28613-8302
(828) 466-2274
E-mail: rogrrabit@webtv.net

American Himalayan Rabbit Club
P.O. Box 37
Sangerfield, NY 13455-0037
(315) 841-4930
E-mail: racota@aol.com

American Netherland Dwarf Rabbit Club
David Pett, Sanction Secretary
17 Ponderey Place
Concord, CA 94521
(925) 687-7656
E-mail: Pettrabbit@aol.com

American Polish Rabbit Club
417 Washington Avenue
Terrace Park, OH 45174
(513) 831-3176

American Sable Rabbit Society
Joyce Gwirtz, Sanction Secretary
6961 Quigg Road
Crestline, OH 44827
(419) 347-1361

American Satin Rabbit Breeders Association
1895 Wilson Avenue
Wilton, IA 52778
(319) 785-6365

American Standard Chinchilla Rabbit Association
7905 Thompson Township Road 81
Bellevue, OH 44811
(419) 483-1009
E-mail: bowman@cros.net

American Tan Rabbit Club
718 CR 216
Sweetwater, TX 79556
(915) 236-4032
E-mail: tanrbt@aol.com